An Illustrated History

America's Patriotic Holidays

John Wesley Thomas & Sandra Lynn Thomas

4880 Lower Valley Road • Atglen, PA 19310

Other Schiffer Books by the Authors:
Thanksgiving and Turkey Collectibles, 0-7643-2092-0, $29.95
Thanksgiving: An Illustrated History, 978-0-7643-3829-8, $29.99
St. Patrick's Day & Irish Collectibles, 978-0-7643-4081-9, $29.99

Other Schiffer Books on Related Subjects:
Holidays and Other Weird Events, 978-0-7643-3362-0, $24.99

Schiffer Books are available at special discounts for bulk purchases for sales promotions or premiums. Special editions, including personalized covers, corporate imprints, and excerpts can be created in large quantities for special needs. For more information contact the publisher:

Published by Schiffer Publishing Ltd.
4880 Lower Valley Road
Atglen, PA 19310
Phone: (610) 593-1777; Fax: (610) 593-2002
E-mail: Info@schifferbooks.com

For the largest selection of fine reference books on this and related subjects, please visit our website at:
www.schifferbooks.com
We are always looking for people to write books on new and related subjects. If you have an idea for a book, please contact us at
proposals@schifferbooks.com

This book may be purchased from the publisher.
Please try your bookstore first.
You may write for a free catalog.

In Europe, Schiffer books are distributed by
Bushwood Books
6 Marksbury Ave.
Kew Gardens
Surrey TW9 4JF England
Phone: 44 (0) 20 8392 8585; Fax: 44 (0) 20 8392 9876
E-mail: info@bushwoodbooks.co.uk
Website: www.bushwoodbooks.co.uk

Copyright © 2012 by John Wesley Thomas & Sandra Lynn Thomas
*Unless otherwise noted, all images are the property of the authors.
Library of Congress Control Number: 2012938681

All rights reserved. No part of this work may be reproduced or used in any form or by any means—graphic, electronic, or mechanical, including photocopying or information storage and retrieval systems—without written permission from the publisher.

The scanning, uploading and distribution of this book or any part thereof via the Internet or via any other means without the permission of the publisher is illegal and punishable by law. Please purchase only authorized editions and do not participate in or encourage the electronic piracy of copyrighted materials.

"Schiffer," "Schiffer Publishing Ltd. & Design," and the "Design of pen and inkwell" are registered trademarks of Schiffer Publishing Ltd.

Designed by RoS
Type set in NewBskvll BT

ISBN: 978-0-7643-4190-8
Printed in China

★ CONTENTS

INTRODUCTION: America's Patriotism at its Best ...4

SECTION ONE: PATRIOTISM AND THE AMERICAN CULTURE
Chapter 1: American Patriotic Music ...22
Chapter 2: America's Revered Icons ...60

SECTION TWO: CELEBRATING AMERICA'S PATRIOTISM
Chapter 3: Independence Day ...96
Chapter 4: President's Day ...122
Chapter 5: Memorial Day (Decoration Day) ...140
Chapter 6: Veteran's Day (Armistice Day) ...154
Chapter 7: Columbus Day ...162
Chapter 8: Labor Day ...168
Chapter 9: Flag Day ...176

BIBLIOGRAPHY ...192

Introduction

America's Patriotism at its Best

Patriotism speaks with a silver tongue. It entices those whose hearts are bursting with nationalistic fervor, but also whose minds forsake the difference between right and wrong. Conversely the trappings of patriotism are rejected by many of those whose inalienable rights are protected at great costs by the blood of unknown patriots.

-- Anonymous

Remembrance of 9-11-01 to signify that our flag shall always wave despite adversities.
Postcard produced by artist and illustrator, Rick of Geary, Carrizozo, New Mexico.

As this book was being written, the 10th Anniversary of 9/11 — the worst terrorist attack on American soil — was being commemorated. It has been generally accepted that this "jihadist" attack was another "wake-up call" to drive home the point that we, as Americans, can never lower our guard in protecting our hard-won freedoms and American democratic traditions. The Global War on Terror, initiated by President George W. Bush on September 17, 2001, has been both directly and indirectly responsible for the termination of three notorious terrorists: (1) Iraq's Saddam Hussein; (2) Osama bin Laden and the shattering of his al-Qaeda terror network; and (3) Libyan dictator Muammar al-Gaddafi. As a consequence the emergence of the "Arab Spring," which were mass demonstrations against other repressive governance throughout parts of North Africa and the Middle East, was gaining substantial momentum.

September 11: Liberty Endures! While 9/11 still invokes mixed emotions of rage and sadness, Americans answered the call to action with a passion and a byword... "We Shall Never Forget!"

However, the first heroes who were responsible for the emergence of America as the world's strongest democracy had its underpinnings through the unselfish behavior of simple, rough-hewn patriots in the mid-eighteenth century. At this time the American colonists were subjects of Great Britain, but, in many respects, were held hostage to the whims of the Crown. The general thought emanating from the Mother Country was that the Americans, though mainly Loyalists, were an independent lot that warranted careful scrutiny and surveillance. Yet these colonists had no representation in the British Parliament and, therefore, no say on the imposition of taxes. While the British Parliament held that the colonists enjoyed "virtual representation," most colonists felt that these taxes were unconstitutional based on the fact that the English Bill of Rights of 1669 had forbidden the imposition of taxes without the consent of Parliament.

In the book *I Hear America Singing*, the authors opined that the first known American published patriotic music appeared in 1768 in *The Boston Gazette*. The tune was the "Liberty Song," which urged:

Come join hand in hand brave Americans all
And rouse your bold hearts at fair Liberty's call.

September 11: Liberty Has Endured! Real time photograph with a view of the Statue of Liberty in the foreground looking toward the Manhattan skyline during the light show emulating from the World Trade Center Towers on September 11, 2011 Memorial. *Photographer: "Joe Sohm/Visions of America /Getty Images." From the author's personal collection.*

"Blondie" Comic Illustration, September 11, 2011. "Never forget...": Dagwood, Blondie, and friends salute the American flag. *Comic by Dean Young and John Marshall.*

The Stamp Act

The events that led up to the penning of this song were the root causes that eventually led to the American Revolutionary War. In 1763, the Seven Years' War, also called the French & Indian War (1754-1763), was finally won by the British with the help of American militias and some Indian tribes, but at great financial cost. As a result of this war, Britain, by receiving Canada from France, confirmed Britain's position as the dominant colonial power in the eastern half of North America. Upon termination of this war, the British Ministry for political reasons, found it necessary to maintain large numbers of British troops on American soil ostensibly to maintain control in the American empire. The only alternative left to finance the massive escalation of these post-war costs (which doubled the British national debt), countered by the fact that political reality made it impossible to further tax British citizens, was to directly tax American colonists. The first of these direct tax measures foisted on the colonies was the SUGAR ACT OF 1764, which levied a surcharge on the importation of foreign molasses in order to favor molasses coming from the British West Indies. However, the next direct tax imposed by the British Parliament, the STAMP ACT OF 1765, was met with great resistance in the American colonies. Heretofore British politicians were taking the position that it should be encumbrant upon the American colonists to contribute a portion to the cost of their defense, but the imposition of such a tax had the potentiality of raising large amounts of revenue without the correlative costs of tax collecting. The Stamp Act required that the majority of printed materials both legal and non-legal used in the colonies be printed on stamped paper produced in Britain carrying an embossed revenue stamp. Additionally it was required that the stamp tax be paid in valid British currency, not in unbacked colonial money.

"Burning of Stamp Act" at Boston, Massachusetts on August, 1765. Lange Series 1, #6. A very early postcard with undivided back; published in the early 1900s.

The Stamp Act, and other prior indirect taxes, gave rise to the well-known slogan "No Taxation without Representation" and its corollary "Taxation without Representation is Tyranny." The American colonists firmly rejected the Stamp Act, which was not only a means for Britain to raise money to reduce its staggering national debt, but also a form of subjugation against the growing restiveness of the colonists.

To enforce these various tax schemes that were highly unpopular with the colonists, the British had to garrison troops in urban centers such as Boston to protect crown-appointed colonial legislative officials. On March 5, 1770, a rowdy mob began to verbally harass one of the sentries stationed near the Old State House in Boston, which was then the seat of British colonial government. The sentry called for help and was reinforced by a small company of British "Redcoats." Further harassment of the soldiers ensued accompanied by the throwing of objects. Without orders the British regulars fired into the crowd, causing five civilian deaths. This unfortunate incident, which was called the "Boston Massacre" or the "Boston Riot" by the British, was well-documented through a colored engraving by Paul Revere. This was one of the main events leading up to the outbreak of the American Revolutionary War in 1775.

The Tea Act of 1773

Likewise another onerous but trivial tax, this time on tea imports, passed under the TEA ACT OF 1773, was the causative factor leading up to the Boston Tea Party on December 16, 1773. In Boston Harbor at Griffin's Wharf lay moored three British ships with cargoes of tea. To defeat King George's tax of three pence a pound, about ninety citizens of Boston disguised as Indians boarded the ships and threw the combined cargoes of 342 chests into the harbor waters. This rebellious act was dramatized by a poetic verse:

> *"No! Ne'er was mingled such a draught*
> *In Palace, Hall or Arbor,*
> *As freemen brewed and Tyrants quaffed,*
> *That Night in Boston Harbor."*

The British Parliament's continued coercive acts of taxation without direct representation was one of the leading causes of the American Revolution that began in 1775 and culminated in the severing of ties with the British Empire with the Declaration of Independence on July 4, 1776.

Advertising Trade Card. "No Taxation Without Representation." Enterprise Coffee, Spice and Drug Mills. The Enterprise Manufacturing Co. of Pa., 1893.

"The Boston Massacre Perpetrated in King Street Boston on March 5th, 1770." Based on a copper engraving by Paul Revere.

"Boston Tea Party Dec 16, 1775." Published by Tuck & Sons; "Independence Day" Series No. 159.

"The Boston Tea Party, State House, Boston, Mass." Published by The Leighton & Valentine Co.

Postcard that features a reproduction of one of the famous murals in the State House at Boston: "Boston Tea Party, December 16, 1773, Boston, Mass."

Shot Heard 'Round the World'

It was the "shot heard 'round the world'" fired by the Patriots against the British regular army "Redcoats" at the Battles of Lexington and Concord on April 19, 1775, that instigated the opening military engagement of the American Revolutionary War. PATRIOTS' DAY has been celebrated in Massachusetts and Maine as a civic or public holiday since 1969 commemorating the anniversary of these episodic battles. Patriotic events have been held such as the reenactment of the "midnight ride" of Paul Revere on April 18, 1775, which was to spread the alarm and warn the "minutemen" in the Lexington and Concord areas that the "British are coming" to seize hidden stores of munitions.

Paul Revere was a prominent silversmith and a colonial militia officer. Based on their experiences in the French and Indian Wars, Revere, along with others, devised a system of intelligence and alarm to keep watch on British military movements. On the night of April 18, 1775, intelligence indicated that the British were unloading troops from transport barges in Boston in order to march to the towns of Lexington and Concord. A prearranged lantern signal (i.e. "one if by land, two if by sea") would indicate the route the British troops would be taking. Throughout that night Revere and many other riders were successful in alerting members of the colonial militia along the 25-mile route that, indeed, the British "Regulars are coming!" The fervor of the heroes of the Revolutionary War spawned numerous patriotic sayings and mottos that still resound today, such as Patrick Henry's "Give me Liberty or Give me Death," Nathan Hale's "I only regret that I have but one life to give for my country," "Live Free or Die," and "Don't Tread On Me," a famous slogan imprinted on the flag carried at the Battle of Bunker Hill.

While the actual fact that American Independence was won at the point of a sword, it was a simple declarative document that gave birth to our nation. In 1774, the First Continental Congress was formed by a hand-picked group of delegates representing all thirteen colonies for the purpose of discussing the thorny issue of the British Crown's insistence of taxation without representation and the British blockade of the Port of Boston in direct response to the Boston Tea Party in 1773. However, the British Parliament did not act to resolve these issues, so the Second Continental Congress was formed in May 1775 to petition King George III to intervene in Parliament on the behalf of the Colonies to rectify certain grievances. Instead, in August, the King issued a proclamation declaring the Colonies to be in a state of "open and avowed rebellion." At this time the Battle of Bunker Hill had just been fought in June.

"Paul Revere's Ride, April 18, 1775." Published by Tuck & Sons; "Independence Day" Series No. 159.

Sheet music "Paul Revere's Ride," published by E. T. Paull, 1905. During his midnight ride, Paul Revere warned other Patriots that the British were marching to Concord.

Color Print of the Works Project Administration: "Minutemen were Patriot soldiers who could be prepared to fight the British in 'a minute.'"

American Revolutionary heroes fight at Bunker Hill under our country's first flag, The Rattlesnake Flag. Postcard published by Winsch.

"Call to Arms – American Revolution." Published by Tuck & Sons; "Independence Day" Series No. 159.

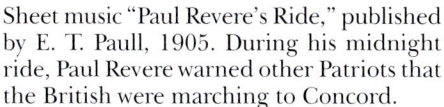
"American Patriots chased British Troops across North Bridge." Original Bettman/Corbis Archives. Reprint 1930s.

"Minute Men American Revolution." Published by Tuck & Sons; "Independence Day" Series No. 159.

The Battle of Bunker Hill

The Battle of Bunker (Breed's) Hill took place on June 17, 1775, during the siege of Boston by colonial troops. The battle was in response to the British wanting to occupy some of the hills surrounding Boston for security purposes. The main contested area, Breed's Hill, was fortified by a colonial militia of about 2,400 soldiers. The British, under General William Howe and with close to 3,000 troops, made three assaults against Breed's and Bunker Hills resulting in a bloody and costly victory for the British. This iconic encounter proved to the British that the colonial troops, if properly led and well-armed, could stand up to regular army troops in varying terrains. While it was a pyrrhic victory for the British with 1,054 killed and wounded compared to 450 militia losses, it showed that the colonial forces would stand and fight for freedom. The Battle also produced another slogan, which was an order issued by one of the American Commanders: "Don't shoot until you see the whites of their eyes."

The Patriots "Viewing the Battle of Bunker Hill" from the rooftops at Charles Town. Published by Tuck & Sons; "Independence Day" Series No. 159.

"The Battle of Bunker Hill." Illustrates the British battle formations in the second assault up Breed's Hill, adjacent to Bunker Hill. Painted by American illustrator Howard Pyle (1853-1911), 1897.

"Battle of Bunker Hill, June 17, 1775." Published by Fred Lounsbury, 1907. Note the slogan on the Pine Tree flag: "An Appeal to Heaven."

Postcard that features a reproduction of one of the famous murals in the State House at Boston: "The Battle of Bunker Hill, June 17, 1775, Charlestown, Mass."

Colonists Claim Independence

After the Battle of Bunker Hill, the Continental Congress realized the need for a standing army to defeat the British troops and established a full-time Continental Army and appointed General George Washington as Commander-in-Chief. After one more year of battles against the entrenched British "Redcoats" and American Loyalist troops, it was decided that American efforts of reconciliation were fruitless. Therefore, on July 4, 1776, the Second Continental Congress at Philadelphia, Pennsylvania, issued a ratified Declaration of Independence, which announced that the thirteen American Colonies regarded themselves as a free, sovereign nation and no longer part of the British Empire; fifty-six delegates to this Continental Congress were signatories of that document. The iconic symbol of American independence, the Liberty Bell, situated in the steeple of the Pennsylvania State House (now renamed Independence Hall) was rung to mark the reading of the Declaration of Independence on July 8, 1776.

"Battle of Bunker Hill." Published by Tuck & Sons; "Independence Day" Series No. 159.

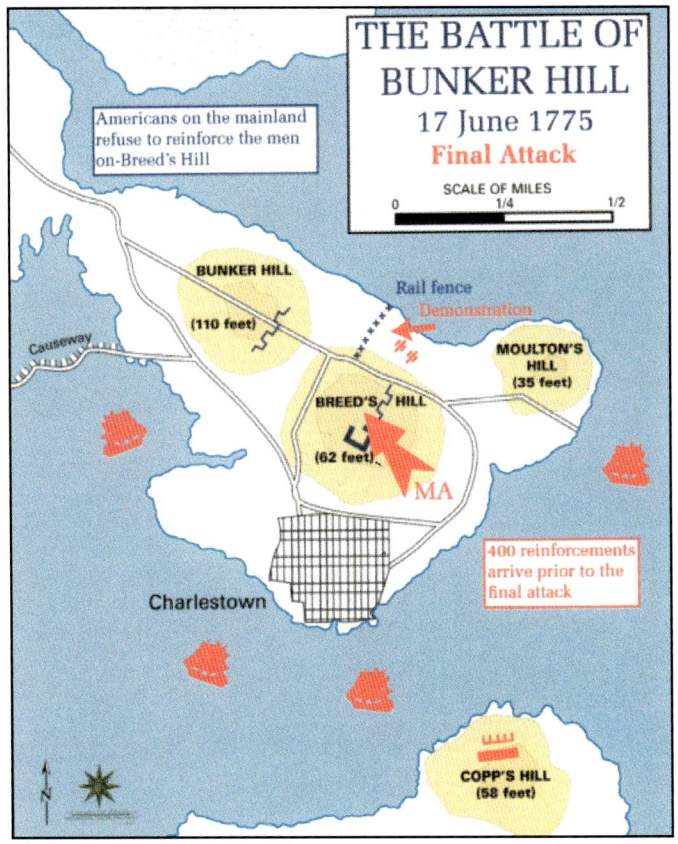

"The Battle of Bunker Hill, 17 June, 1775-Final Attack." This map shows the last positions of the Patriots and the British troops at the final assault.

"Washington taking command of the Army" on June 14, 1775 when Congress formed the new Continental Army. Soldiers salute Washington as their Commander-in-Chief. Publisher unknown.

Since 1776, the birthday of the new United States of America has been celebrated every July 4th as Independence Day, the first of many American Patriotic celebrations and holidays. Based on the legendary heroics of battles leading up to the Declaration of Independence, an Ohio-based American painter, Archibald MacNeal Willard, in 1875 painted the iconic Revolutionary War scene of two drummers and a fife player marching at the head of colonial troops. This painting, first called "Yankee Doodle," is now known as "The Spirit of '76."

"Framing the Declaration of Independence." Published by Tuck & Sons; "Independence Day" Series No. 159.

"Signing of the Declaration of Independence." After the Declaration of Independence was signed in 1776, Congress resolved that one flag be made for all the United States. Published by Ticnor Bros., Inc.; "Flag Series" No. 14.

"Independence Hall, Philadelphia." Published by Tuck & Sons; "Independence Day" Series No. 159.

"The Declaration of Independence." Published by Tuck & Sons; "Independence Day" Series No. 109.

"Independence Hall and Liberty Bell." Published by Tuck & Sons; "Independence Day" Series No. 109.

"The First Fourth of July." Published by Tuck & Sons; "Independence Day" Series No. 109.

"The Spirit of '76." Published by Tuck & Sons; "Independence Day" Series No. 109.

"Yankee Doodle or The Spirit of '76." Painted by Archibald MacNeal Willard. Publisher unknown.

General George Washington

In the next six years there were approximately twenty noteworthy battles that led the combined American and then the Franco-American forces under General George Washington to finally defeat the British occupying armed forces. These included the Battle of Long Island on August 27, 1776 (the first major battle of the war) and the Battles of Trenton and Princeton, New Jersey. It was at the Battle of Trenton that a famous iconic painting of Revolutionary American history was made by Samuel Leutze in 1851 depicting General George Washington majestically standing on the bow of a rowboat crossing the Delaware River to successfully attack the Hessian mercenary forces on Christmas Day, 1776. The Americans killed twenty-two Hessians, wounded ninety-eight, and captured nearly nine hundred while only losing three of their own men in horrific weather conditions. As a sidebar many historians have pointed out several errors in this painting. The most serious error was the fact that Washington would not have used the earliest "stars-and-stripes" flag as it was not adopted until 1777. Still this beautiful painting is a patriotic symbol of the efforts to bring freedom to an embryonic country. Washington followed up this victory with another successful attack against British troops at the Battle of Princeton on January 3, 1777.

A major victory for the Continental Army was the defeat and capture of more than 6,000 British troops under General John Burgoyne at the Battle of Saratoga on October 17, 1777. It was in the aftermath of this victory that Congress proclaimed the first National Day for solemn Thanksgiving and praise on December 18, 1777. Very soon after General Washington moved his poorly fed and ill-equipped army of 12,000 Continentals into winter quarters at Valley Forge, Pennsylvania. During the six months at Valley Forge, nearly 4,000 troops were declared unfit for duty (only one-third of them had shoes) and 2,500 died from multiple diseases. On February 23, 1778, the German Baron Von Steuben joined Washington's staff and offered his military skills as a drill instructor to carry out an effective training program. This was accomplished and, when the newly refurbished Continental Army paraded on May 6, 1778, it was to celebrate the new French alliance with America.

"Holding the Line – Continental Army." Published by Tuck & Sons; "Independence Day" Series No. 159.

"Ragged Continentals." Published by Tuck & Sons; "Independence Day" Series No. 109.

"Washington Crossing the Delaware, Dec 25, 1776." Published by Tuck & Sons; "George Washington's Birthday" Series No. 124.

General George Washington reviews his ragged and hungry troops at the Valley Forge, Pennsylvania, winter encampment. Published by William L. Trego, Valley Forge Historical Society.

"Who helped to make us free? Washington." Gen. George Washington crosses the icy water of the Delaware River. Published by International Art Publishing Co.; Series 51646. Postcard is based on a painting by Samuel Leutze.

"Washington at the Battle of Princeton." Washington and his troops attacked the British garrison January 1, 1777. Published by Tuck & Sons; "Washington's Birthday" Series No. 156.

"Washington at Valley Forge." Artist signed R. Veenfliet. Publisher unknown; Series No. 51766.

"Valley Forge Dec. 1777." On December 19, 1777, 12,000 soldiers arrived in Valley Forge and began to build shelter. Severe conditions with little food, inadequate clothing, and crowded damp quarters resulted in sickness and death. Diseases killed over 2,500 men that winter. After a six-month encampment, Washington left the area and marched to New York. Published by Tuck & Sons; "Independence Day" Series No. 159.

"First in War, First in Peace, First in the Hearts of his Countrymen." George Washington salutes his soldiers at Valley Forge. Published by M. W. Taggart; Series 605.

Soon after, at the Battle of Monmouth, New Jersey, on June 28, 1778, the famous legend of Molly Pitcher (based on true facts) ensued. During the battle, which was the largest one-day battle in the war, "Molly Pitcher," who was the wife of one of the soldiers, delivered water to the thirsty combatants as it was a stifling hot day. She also used the water to swab down the cannons with wet rags after each firing sequence after her husband, one of the gunners, became wounded.

"If George Washington could see us now!" Artist signed HBG (HB Griggs). Published by L. & E.; Series 2242.

"Molly Pitcher at the Cannon's Mouth." Published by Tuck & Sons; "Independence Day" Series No. 159.

After three more years of battles, the combined Franco-American forces of 19,000 under General George Washington and the Comte de Rochambeau defeated General Lord Charles Cornwallis with 9,000 forces during the Siege of Yorktown, Virginia, that ended on October 17, 1781. Due to the Treaty of Paris, which was signed by American and British representatives on September 3, 1783, the British Government acknowledged the independence of the United States. This treaty ended the American Revolutionary War. At this time, the British Government ordered the evacuation of their last stronghold, New York City, and this agreed upon date was November 25, 1783. Therefore, this day has been called "Evacuation Day." When it was apparent that the last vestige of British authority had departed New York, General George Washington, with a flotilla of boats, entered New York harbor. After this moment in history, the majority of the Continental army, navy, and marines were demobilized. It was the adoption of the American Constitution by "plain, honest men" on September 17, 1788, that gave Congress the power to "raise and support armies," "provide and maintain a navy," and to "make rules for the Government and the regulation of the land and naval forces," as well as the power "to declare war." These powers would come in useful in a short period of time.

"The Girl Behind the Gun." The postcard is based on Molly Pitcher. Publisher unknown.

"Memories of the War of Independence – The Surrender of Cornwallis at Yorktown – October 19, 1781.'" Published by Fred Lounsbury in 1907.

"Washington Entering New York." Published by Tuck & Sons; "Washington's Birthday" Series No. 156.

"Reception of President Washington at New York" and "Washington taking oath of office as President." Published by Tuck & Sons; "George Washington's Birthday" Series No. 124.

"Washington's Inauguration as President." Published by Tuck & Sons "Washington's Birthday" Series No. 156.

"Washington at Yorktown." Washington overlooks the battlefield from a redoubt. Postcard is based on an illustration by R. Veenfliet. Publisher unknown; Series No. 51766.

From the Declaration of Independence in 1776 to the throwing off the yoke of British imperialism in 1783 by the defeat of its armed forces, American Patriots, for the next six years in the absence of a barely functioning government, were able to muster enough resolve to write the Constitution, formulate the Bill of Rights, and elect the "Father of Our Country" — General George Washington, the first President of the United States — in 1789. Washington's Birthday is celebrated as a Federal holiday annually in February, also unofficially known as President's Day, which includes the birthday of President Abraham Lincoln.

While not a Federal holiday, CONSTITUTION DAY (or Citizenship Day) is an American federal observance that recognizes the adoption and ratification of the United States Constitution as well as those who have become U. S. citizens. It is celebrated on the nearest weekday to September 17th in any given year. While the first recognition of Constitution Day goes back to the 1900s, it was only in 2004 that a law was established creating a federal holiday observance. Schools that receive federal funds of any kind must provide instruction on the history of the American Constitution on that day.

Celebrating CONSTITUTION DAY. Produced by Founders of America, 1955.

Fruit Crate Label: "Constitution." Frances Citrus Assn., Frances, California. Dated 1928.

Patriotism is deeply embedded in the American culture as witnessed by the number of patriotic-themed Federal holidays we celebrate. From 1620, when the Pilgrims first set foot on American soil, to nearly four hundred years later, Americans again will invoke their constitutional rights to freely elect, by popular vote, the forty-fifth President of the United States. INAUGURATION DAY, another Federal holiday held every fourth year following the Presidential election, will take place on January 20, 2013.

"George Washington-Father of His Country": GEORGE WASHINGTON'S BIRTHDAY. Published by Winsch. Date and series unknown.

"Lincoln the President" signs the Emancipation Proclamation… "The Noblest Deed of all": ABRAHAM LINCOLN'S BIRTHDAY. Published by The Rose Company, 1908.

DECORATION DAY: Soldiers from 1776 to 1900 are proudly shown in their uniforms under the flag they for which they fought and the laurel wreath of victory. Published by Winsch; "Decoration Day" Series No. 3.

MEMORIAL DAY: "In Memory of our Heroes." Lady Liberty, draped by a flag, holds out a crown of laurel leaves. The fallen brave soldiers are honored in the background. Artist is C. Chapman. Published by International Art Publishing Company.

FOURTH OF JULY postcard: A child, proudly dressed as a Patriot, celebrates Independence Day with flags and fireworks. Artist signed Bernhardt Wall. Published by Ullman Manufacturing Co.; "Independence Day" Series No. 122.

FLAG DAY postcard: A group of schoolboys cheer the red, white, and blue (flag). Published by A.S.B.; Series No. 283.

Patriotism

And the American Culture

Section One

Chapter 1

American Patriotic Music

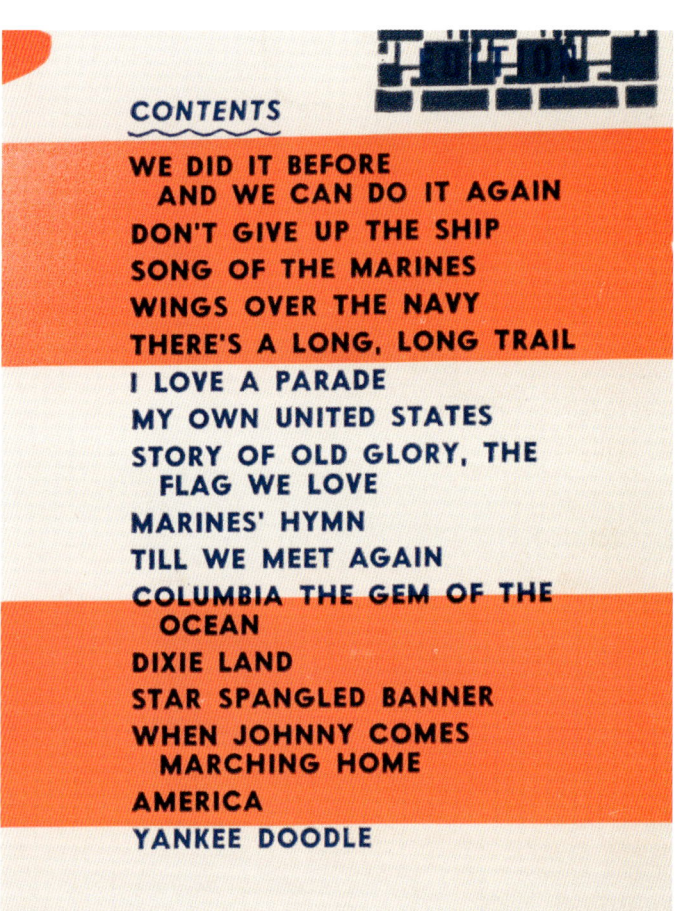

Song book *America Patriotic Songs*, with front cover listing sixteen old favorites.

America, from its earliest beginnings, has experienced a tumultuous history befitting a country approaching maturation. In the throes of preserving and protecting our country's democratic traditions, America's citizens, like it or not, have had to fight many bloody wars in many regions of the world. In one fashion or another many of these battles and wars were provoked by outside enemies except the American Civil War, which was a catastrophe in of itself.

Nonetheless, each of these conflicts produced notable patriotic slogans and songs. It has been estimated that more than 10,000 melodies and songs were inspired by the Civil War while 9,700 songs were published during America's short involvement in World War I. America's participation in World War II was longer, but produced a much smaller number of songs in that creative songsmiths produced songs to help the war effort. However, most had little commercial value. Post-World War II conflicts produced little of patriotic merit as a more sophisticated citizenry was now becoming disillusioned with far-flung engagements that bore little threats to the homeland. However,

September 11, 2001 (or 9/11 as it is often referenced) changed that attitude — more than ten years later America is still reeling from the horrific effects of homicidal terrorism on its own soil.

Patriotism is a sentiment that is expressed as love of and/or devotion to one's country. It may take the form of slogans, quotes, poetry, and songs all spoken, sung, or written in the vernacular with a dialect common to a particular region. For example, many patriotic songs of the South used a dialect wording that would be construed as African-American Vernacular English. Patriotic music, therefore, uses songs, hymns, lyrics, and music from theatrical venues to espouse sentiment and passion for the ideal of national unity...usually in times of peril.

Throughout America's relatively short history, nation-building episodic events have occurred that inspired songwriters to create melodies and lyrics to elevate the human spirit for their love of country. For the most part domestic patriotic music has been born out of necessity due to the instigation of a revolution, secession, and civil war, as well as wars foisted on America from abroad. Within the purview of this book the six main warring events through the 1940s were (1) the American Revolutionary War or the War of Independence; (2) the War of 1812; (3) the American Civil War; (4) the Spanish-American War; (5) World War I; and (6) World War II.

Up to a point in time, circa 1750s and 1760s, the American colonists were British citizens and subject to British rule. As tensions between the American colonies and the British government mounted due to the British's imposition of taxes, one form of protests involved the use of resistance songs and parodies usually set to the tune of an existing song. The one song that had official weighting among the British colonists was "God Save the King." First introduced in print in 1745 but known earlier, this song (melody and lyrics) was considered to be the national anthem of Great Britain and of the Colonies. The abbreviated lines of the first stanza are:

> *God save great George our king, Long live our noble king.*
> *Long to reign over us, God save the king.*
> *God save the king. Send him victorious, Happy and victorious.*

Composite Postcard: "God Save the King." Lyrics: Author Unknown; Music: Thomas Augustine Arne. First published in *The Gentleman's Magazine*, October 15, 1745.

And as the 1750s segued into the 1760s, a broadening rift among citizens within the thirteen original colonies was becoming more apparent. Those who maintained fidelity to the British crown were termed "Loyalist/Tories" while those who were becoming more disenchanted with the onerous actions of the crown were called "Patriots/Whigs." Therefore, to the tune of "God Save the King," the patriots issued many forms of parodies that savagely mocked the crown. Eventually, however, the stirring tune, not the lyrics, of "God Save the King" found its way into the mainstream of American song books. As an example, this tune was put with lyrics to "God Save Great Washington" for his birthday in 1784, as well as becoming the basis for another well-known patriotic song, "My Country 'Tis of Thee," published in 1831.

Yankee Doodle

The most famous song to arise out of the Revolutionary War was the simple tune "Yankee Doodle," based on an old nursery rhyme. From historic perspective, the genesis of this song is attributed to a British Army surgeon who, upon witnessing the appearance and conduct of the American colonial troops during the French and Indian Wars, wrote verses that mocked the disorganized "Yankees." Like the song, "God Save the King," the verses of "Yankee Doodle" have been shanghaied by both the colonial troops and the British to serve their purpose of taunting each other's wartime activities. While there are many versions of "Yankee Doodle," the most common verse and refrain was:

An 1894 Patriotic song sheet for "Yankee Doodle." Published by Elliott Publishing Co. Original.

Yankee Doodle went to town
Riding on a pony,
He stuck a feather in his hat,
And called it macaroni.

According to linguists, the derivation of the word "doodle" comes from Low German, a West Germanic language family, meaning a fool or simpleton. With respect to the fashionistas of that period, "macaroni" was an extreme style of wig. Therefore, the implication of the verse was that the Yankees were so simple and naïve that sticking a feather in their hat somehow made them more cultured and acceptable.

A famous oil painting made one hundred years later by Archibald MacNeal Willard, circa 1875, was titled "Yankee Doodle" or "The Spirit of '76" commemorated American independence with an iconic scene of two drummers and a fifer in the heat of battle. Fast forward to 1942, when "Yankee Doodle" was featured in a famous dance sequence in *Yankee Doodle Dandy*, the Warner Brothers film starring James Cagney as George M. Cohan in a biographical musical tribute to Hollywood's famous song-and-dance man.

Song sheet for "Let's be Ready! That's the Spirit of '76." Music was composed by Chas. Bayra and Rubey Cowel in 1916.

"Yankee Doodle": The drum and fife trio march to the music. Illustrated is the first stanza. Published by Charles Rose; Series 11/5.

"Yankee Doodle": A young patriot proudly plays the drum while celebrating. Published by L. R. Conwell; Series No. 383.

"Yankee Doodle." Published by GDD; Series No. 2032.

Hail Columbia

After the birth of our nation in 1776, the first true patriotic song, "Hail Columbia," was composed by Philip Phile in 1789 for the inauguration of the first President of the United States, George Washington. It was originally meant to be a musical march, but lyrics were added in 1798. For more than one hundred years, "Hail Columbia," with some other patriotic songs, was the de facto national anthem as the name Columbia represented the United States, mainly to Europeans. While there were at least four stanzas, the first of ten lines and its chorus are the best known:

"Hail Columbia – Memorial Day Souvenir," publisher unknown.

Hail Columbia, happy land!
Hail, ye heroes, heav'n-born band,
Who fought and bled on freedom's cause,
Who fought and bled on freedom's cause,
And when the storm of war was gone
Enjoy'd the peace your valor won.
Let independence be our boast,
Ever mindful what it cost;
Ever grateful for the prize,
Let its altar reach its skies.
(Chorus)
Firm, united let us be,
Rallying round our liberty,
As a band of brothers joined,
Peace and safety we shall find.

The Star-Spangled Banner

The ignominious and decisive defeat of General Cornwallis and the British Army by a combined American and French land and naval forces at Yorktown, Virginia, on October 19, 1781 proved to be the last major land war of the American Revolution. This result led to the eventual signing of the Treaty of Paris on September 3, 1783, which formally ended the American Revolutionary War between Great Britain and the United States of America and its allies. This treaty was ratified on January 14, 1784, giving rise to a minor annual observance, called RATIFICATION DAY, which established the United States as a sovereign entity. One of the articles of the Treaty "acknowledged the United States to be free, sovereign, and independent states" and declares the intention of both parties to "secure to both perpetual peace and harmony."

Unfortunately, most of the promises were one-sided, and for most of the next twenty-nine years, the British navy harassed American shipping on the high seas by excluding them from trading with the British colonies in the West Indies. Also, American ships were stopped and searched, with cargo at times being removed and some of the sailors impressed into the British navy. President James Madison realized that war was, again, inevitable with Britain, mainly between naval forces on both the Atlantic/Gulf, the Great Lakes, and other navigable bodies of water on the British-North American frontier. As a result of British predilections against America shipping, President Madison declared war on the British on June 18, 1812. At this time the United States Navy consisted of twenty frigates while Britain had more than 1,000 men-of-war at her disposal.

USA Commemorative 44-cent postage stamp recognizing the ratification of the Treaty of Paris on January 14, 1784.

The War of 1812 provided America with its greatest and most popular patriotic song. The story of "The Star-Spangled Banner" is well known, but here is a brief account: On September 13, 1814, a lawyer by the name of Francis Scott Key was sent on a mission by President Madison to visit the British fleet stationed in Chesapeake Bay to work out the details for an exchange of prisoners. However, Key and his companion were detained on the British vessel overnight because they were aware of the British plans to shell Baltimore. During the night Key witnessed the sustained bombardment of Fort McHenry, one of Baltimore's defensive forts. However, he was not able to ascertain the outcome of the battle until dawn…when he happily observed the large American flag still flying over the fort. This flag, with fifteen stars and fifteen stripes, became known as the Star-Spangled Banner Flag. Key was so inspired by the American rejection of the British's plans to capture Baltimore that he wrote a poem to commemorate the triumphant occasion. After his release on September 16th, Key finished the poem, which he called the "Defense of Fort McHenry." Shortly thereafter Key's brother-in-law matched the poem, ironically, to a popular British melody "The Anacreontic Song," a drinking song sung by amateur musicians. By September 20th, local newspapers printed the song along with the suggestion that the words could be sung to the tune…"Anacreon in Heaven." Days later a music dealer published the words and music together under the title "The Star-Spangled Banner."

The culmination of the War of 1812 ended with the signing of the Treaty of Ghent (Belgium) on December 24, 1814, which was ratified by Congress on February 16, 1815. However, between these dates one of the most bloodiest and decisive victories of the war by the Americans occurred at the Battle of New Orleans on January 8, 1815. In what was probably the most famous land battle of the war, Major General Andrew Jackson (aka "Old Hickory"), with a diverse force of over 4,000 U. S. regular troops, rural militiamen, and Choctaw Indian tribesmen, defeated a much larger force of 11,000 British regular troops. This battle, and the resultant end of the war, enhanced Andrew Jackson's reputation, which eventually culminated in him being elected as the country's seventh president.

"The Star Spangled Banner." Published by Winsch; "National Song" Series.

"The Star Spangled Banner." Published by L. R. Conwell; No. 386.

"Watchful-Waiting – The Star Spangled Banner: By these colors we stand ever true… Three Cheers for the Red, White, and Blue." Published by Henry Heininger Co.

As an aside, in 1959 the comedic song "The Battle of New Orleans" sung by Johnny Horton reached the top of the Billboard charts. While the Americans did not secure a resolution on many of the needed maritime rights, the war validated the Louisiana Purchase (from France on July 4, 1803) and also completed the fight for independence that began at the Lexington-Concord battle of 1775 some forty years prior. In July 1889, the U.S. Navy officially began using "The Star-Spangled Banner" at flag-raising ceremonies, a practice copied by the Army. The four-stanza song, despite its difficulty in singing due to its octave range, gained great popularity throughout the nineteenth century with bands, both military and civilian, playing it at civic events and Independence Day celebrations.

However, until President Herbert Hoover signed a law on March 3, 1931, adopting "The Star-Spangled Banner" as the national anthem of the United States, other patriotic songs such as "Hail Columbia" and "My Country, 'Tis of Thee" were all considered to be acceptable unofficial anthems of our country. Perhaps not well-known is the fact that the seldom sung fourth stanza of our national anthem includes the line: "And this be our motto: In God is our Trust." In 1956, the United States Congress adopted "In God We Trust" as the country's national motto. In present time, whenever the National Anthem is sung, know it or not, Americans are still commemorating the War of 1812.

Painting of General Andrew Jackson as he lifts his sword to encourage the defenders against British General Edward Pakenham during a battle near New Orleans, January 8, 1815. Neither leader realized the war was officially over as the Treaty of Ghent was already signed. Original painting by Edward Percy Moran, 1910.

Postcard of original painting now located in Toledo Museum of Art.

My Country 'Tis of Thee

The next two American patriotic songs were born not out of conflicts, but by inspiration based on the melodies of two famous British anthems. In 1831, the lyrics to "My Country 'Tis of Thee" were written by Samuel Francis Smith based on the melody of Great Britain's "God Save the Queen (or King)." The song was first performed on July 4, 1831, for an Independence Day celebration, and the words and melody were then published under the name "America" in 1832. In 1904, when a melody was added to the poem "American the Beautiful," this caused some confusion with the original named "America" so "My Country 'Tis of Thee" became the name of choice. Of the four original stanzas, the first is obviously the best known and, when sung, the first and fourth stanzas appear to be the most popular:

My country 'tis of thee,
Sweet land of liberty,
Of thee I sing;
Land where my father's died,
Land of the pilgrim's pride,
From ev'ry mountainside
Let freedom ring!

"My Country 'Tis of Thee." Published by M. W. Taggart; Series No. 602.

Three additional verses were added to the melody over time and, in 1843, Abolitionists co-opted the melody to add six additional verses for an anti-slavery theme. This song, if not already famous, was made so by a rendition by Marian Anderson, an African-American contralto, sung on Easter Sunday, April 9, 1939, in front of 75,000 spectators on the steps of the Lincoln Memorial in Washington, D.C.

Uncle Sam and a Canadian Mountie compare "My Country 'Tis of Thee" and "God Save the King" – they're the same tune and the same colors." Published by G. M. Rose, The Department of Agriculture, Canada.

Columbia, Gem of the Ocean

The next in the chronological line of American patriotic songs is "Columbia, the Gem of the Ocean." Also known as the "Red, White, and Blue," it was composed by David T. Shaw in 1843. While there has been confusion as to the real lyricist, it is now generally believed, according to sheet music publications, that Shaw was given credit as the composer and Thomas a' Becket was the arranger. Nonetheless, the song bears a strong resemblance to a British patriotic song, "Britannia, the Pride of the Ocean." Interestingly, both songs utilize heroic feminine symbols such as Columbia for the United States and Britannia for Great Britain as well as the same melody. While this song was considered also to be one of two or three other unofficial national anthems, the words today are not well known and rarely sung. The song consists of three verses, of which the first is:

O Columbia! The gem of the ocean,
The home of the brave and the free,
The shrine of each patriot's devotion,
A world offers homage to thee;
Thy mandates make heroes assemble,
When Liberty's form stands in view;
Thy banners make tyranny tremble,
When borne by the red, white and blue…

This song remained popular up to the American Civil War when this fratricidal conflict produced thousands of songs written across a spectrum from inspiration to mockery.

"Columbia the Gem of the Ocean." Published by Winsch; "National Song" Series.

"Columbia the Gem of the Ocean." Published by Charles Rose; Series 11/17.

"The Red, White, and Blue." Published by M. W. Taggart; Series No. 602.

The American Civil War

The American Civil War's hostilities began April 12, 1861, when Confederate forces attacked a U.S. military installation at Fort Sumter, South Carolina. Essentially this war was fought by eleven secessionist Southern states (The Confederacy) in an effort to continue and expand slavery for economic needs while the twenty-five Northern and Western states fought to preserve the union while controlling the growth of slavery. One of the innovations to come out from this war was the first offensive use of armored ships, which changed global naval warfare forever. At the Battle of Hampton Roads, Virginia, in March 1862, the *CCS Virginia* (the former *USS Merrimack*), in an effort to break the Union blockade of two Southern ports, met up with the *USS Monitor*, an iron-clad gunboat. After several hours during which the cannon fire directed at each other had little impact, the battle was called off with no clear victor. Two months later the *Merrimack* was scuttled and, at the end of 1862, the *Monitor* sank in high seas. After four years of ground and naval battles, the "bloodiest war" in our nation's history came to an end by the surrender of Confederate General Robert E. Lee to Union General Ulysses S. Grant at Appomattox Court House, Virginia, on April 9, 1865.

"The Monitor's Great Victory." Published by Winsch; Series unknown.

"Destruction of the Merrimac." Published by A. C. Boselman & Co.; Series unknown.

Ulysses S. Grant, General of the Union Army. There are twenty-five stars on the flag canton. Publisher unknown.

Postcard of General Robert E. Lee with Confederate States of America flag as backdrop. Publisher unknown.

Lincoln and the Gettysburg Address

During this civil war, President Abraham Lincoln not only issued his Emancipation Proclamation on January 1, 1863, essentially freeing 3.1 million slaves in all states, union or not, but also gave what is considered to be one of the finest speeches in United States history: his Gettysburg Address. The occasion of Lincoln's speech on November 19, 1863, was the dedication of the Soldiers' National Cemetery at Gettysburg, Pennsylvania, where 3,513 Union dead were interred — the result of the Battle of Gettysburg, fought from July 1-3, 1863, between the forces of Union General Meade's Army of the Potomac and General Lee's Army of Northern Virginia. The three-day battle contributed the largest casualties of the entire American Civil War and resulted in the defeat of Lee's forces, which ended his invasion of the North. It is estimated that both sides had a combined 46,286 killed, wounded, and captured or missing in just this battle while the entire campaign, which ended on July 27th, had an estimated 57,225 casualties; that figure exceeds all of the dead and wounded suffered during the eight years of the American Revolutionary War. President Lincoln's Gettysburg Address, though only ten sentences long, honored the fallen dead and redefined the purpose of the war as a new birth of freedom that would bring equality to all citizens and ensure that there still would be representative democracy. Lincoln's stirring words still resounds deeply today:

"We here highly resolve that these dead shall not have died in vain — that this nation, under God, shall have a new birth of freedom — and that the government of the people, by the people, and for the people shall not perish from the earth."

Just five days after the American Civil War ended, President Lincoln was assassinated on April 14, 1865, by John Wilkes Booth as Lincoln and his wife watched a play at Ford's Theatre in Washington D.C. Booth was subsequently tracked down, shot, and killed on April 26, 1865. In order to honor the memory of the 16th President of the United States, the Lincoln Memorial, located on the National Mall opposite the Washington Monument, was dedicated May 30, 1922, with the central figure — a seated Lincoln — nineteen feet tall. Located in Springfield, Illinois, at the Oak Ridge Cemetery, is Lincoln's Tomb (Monument), which is Lincoln's final resting place as well as his wife, Mary Todd Lincoln, and three of their four sons. Built from 1868 to 1874, the memorial consists of a 117-foot high obelisk set on a rectangular base.

"Abraham Lincoln presenting the Proclamation of Freedom to a Slave." Artist signed C. Chapman. Published by International Art Publishing Co.; Series No. 51818.

"Lincoln's Address at Gettysburg." Published by Tuck & Sons; "Lincoln's Birthday" Series No. 155.

"Lincoln Monument Springfield, Illinois." Published by Tuck & Sons; "Lincoln's Birthday" Series No. 155.

Civil War Era Songs

During this four-year fratricidal war, song writers and composers contributed some 10,000 songs with the far majority forgotten forever. However, at least six songs are still well-remembered today, if not still sung occasionally, with one having a somewhat tarnished reputation. In 1861, two of the most sung and memorable songs of the war were written; one for the Union and one for the Confederacy.

Battle Hymn of the Republic

Probably the most stirring song that evolved from the Union side of the Civil War and has been subsequently sung over the course of three more wars was the very popular "Battle Hymn of the Republic." Like many songs of the era, the melody was composed by one person while another person provided the lyrics; usually with some passage of time between the two occurrences. With the "Battle Hymn," the tune or melody was first written in 1856 by William Steffe, which was matched with campfire spiritual lyrics. In 1860, the popular lyrics of "John Brown's Body" were matched with Steffe's melody to produce another very popular song although abolitionist in nature. In November 1861, the poet and social activist Julia Ward Howe visited President Lincoln in Washington D.C. At a review of marching Union troops, a friend suggested that she write new lyrics to the "John Brown's Body" melody. Within a day or two, Howe wrote the lyrics and those combined with Steffe's music was published as the "Battle Hymn of the Republic" in the February 1862 edition of the *Atlantic Monthly*. As an aside, Julia Ward Howe was responsible for the first proclamation of "Mother's Day" in 1870. The popular and best-known first stanza out of six is:

"Battle Hymn of the Republic." Published by E. Nash; "National Song" Series.

Mine eyes have seen the glory of the coming of the Lord:
He is trampling out the vintage where the grapes of wrath are stored;
He hath loosed the fateful lighting of His terrible swift sword:
His truth is marching on.
(Chorus now sings)
Glory, glory, hallelujah!
Glory, glory, hallelujah!
Glory, glory, hallelujah!
His truth is marching on.

While most of the six stanzas contain Biblical references, the very popular melody has been used for years with different lyrics in many secular venues.

Dixie's Land

Another widely popular American song (and eventually among the most controversial) during the mid-nineteenth century had its underpinnings due to blackface minstrelsy. This song had various names such as "Dixie," "I Wish I Was In Dixie," and "Dixie's Land." The very interesting story of how this "walk-around" song was created is available on many websites. However, learned musicologists credit Northern-born Daniel Decatur Emmett as the sole originator of the song's composition circa 1859. Since the song had its origins in the North, it first became very popular in the many blackface minstrel touring shows in and around the large population centers of the Northeast. At that time, in face of growing abolitionist sentiment, minstrel shows performed songs such as "Dixie," which, purposeful or not, portrayed slavery as a positive institution. Hence, if you read any of the countless lyrics of "Dixie," you will realize that the song's protagonist, the pining ex-black slave, is not finding freedom to his liking and wishes to be back to his old plantation:

"Dixie for the Union" song sheet. Words by Frances J. Crosby; melody by Dan S, Emmett. "On ye patriots to the battle, Hear Fort Moultrie's cannon rattle; Then away, then away, then away to the fight! Go, meet those Southern traitors, with iron will. And should your courage falter, boys, remember Bunker Hill. Hurrah! Hurrah! Hurrah!" Original. 1861.

I wish I was in the land of cotton,
Old times they are not forgotten;
Look away! Look away! Look away! Dixie Land.
In Dixie Land where I was born,
Early on one frosty mornin,
Look away! Look away! Look away! Dixie Land.

As the American Civil War began, Southern sympathizers introduced "Dixie" to the South, where, not only did it become an instant favorite, but it also became the "unofficial" National Anthem of the Confederate States of America. Both Union and Confederate lyricists produced not only patriotic versions for their own uses, but also parodies of each other's efforts. The etymological background of the word "Dixie" is varied, but, regardless of its originality, the word remains a synonym or nickname for the South.

The appropriation of the song "Dixie" by the South irritated the Northerners, so songwriters, Daniel Decatur Emmett among them, composed forgettable songs such as "Dixie For the Union" and "Dixie Unionized." These songs could be found in the repertoire of Union and civilian bands for several years during the Civil War, but eventually passed out of favor. Sometime after the war, "Dixie Doodle Girl" was written, along with patriotic graphics, to express closure and bring "Dixie" back into acceptance by Northern interests.

"Dixie Doodle Girl" song sheet. March Two-Step (no words): Music by W. C. Powell; Artist Bertha Youngs. Original. 1916.

Battle Cry of Freedom

In 1862 a true Union patriotic song, the "Battle Cry of Freedom," was written and composed by George F. Root. Because the song so passionately espoused the cause of the Union, the spirited verse spurred the sales of over 700,000 sheet music copies in the North alone. Due to the rampant popularity of this song, the Confederates co-opted the melody and added their version of lyrics, which supported the Southern cause. The first stanza of the Union version of this rousing four-stanza song is:

Yes, we'll rally round the flag, boys, we'll rally once again,
Shouting the battle cry of freedom,
We will rally from the hillside, we'll gather from the plain,
Shouting the battle cry of freedom!
(Chorus)
The Union forever! Hurrah, boys, hurrah!
Down with the traitor, up with the star;
While we rally around the flag, boys, rally once again,
Shouting the battle cry of freedom!

"I Wish I Was in Dixie's Land" sheet music cover. Lyrics by Dan D. Emmett. Arranged by W. L. Hobbs. 1861.

"In Dixie's Land." Published by GDD; Series No. 2032.

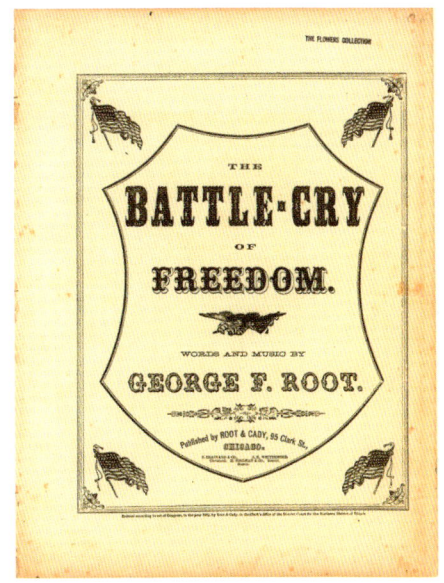

"The Battle Cry of Freedom" sheet music cover. Words and music by George F. Root, 1862.

"The Battle Cry of Freedom" by George F. Root (August 30, 1820–August 6, 1895), 1862.

When Johnny Comes Marching Home Again

The mid-point of the Civil War occurred in 1863 with the tide shifting over to the North. There were four major battles fought; each had combined losses of more than 30,000 troops with Gettysburg having the largest at 45,000. Due to the carnage of these battles, many of the patriotic songs were evocative of the changes in war sentiment. Songs such as "Just Before the Battle Mother," "Mother Would Comfort Me," "Weeping Sad and Lonely" were hardly rousing patriotic songs. However, the most popular song of that year, "When Johnny Comes Marching Home Again," reflected people's hope for the safe and speedy return of their relatives and friends fighting the war. The lyrics were written by Louis Lambert, a pseudonym of an Irish-American band leader, Patrick Gilmore. Supposedly the melody was adapted from an Irish anti-war song. Gilmore wrote four stanzas, of which the first is:

When Johnny comes marching home again
Hurrah! Hurrah!
We'll give him a hearty welcome then
Hurrah! Hurrah!
The men will cheer and the boys will shout
The ladies they will all turn out
And we'll all feel gay
When Johnny comes marching home.

Because of the motivational aspects in the wording of the verses implying relief for those surviving the war, the song was sung by both sides.

"When Johnny Comes Marching Home" sheet music cover. Words and music by Louis Lambert. 1863.

Tramp! Tramp! Tramp! The Prisoners Hope

The Confederate forces had their share of victories that resulted in captured prisoners during 1863 and 1864. When a scheduled prisoner exchange broke down, the Confederates had to hastily build a prisoner-of-war camp in Andersonville, Georgia, in early 1864. This open-air facility, built to hold 10,000 prisoners, ended up, by the end of the war, housing more than 45,000 captives of which nearly 13,000 died in captivity. An equally notorious prisoner facility in Elmira, New York, held Confederate prisoners under almost the same heinous conditions. Due to these abysmal conditions, a Northern songwriter, George F. Root (who also wrote the "The Battle Cry of Freedom"), composed one of the most popular martial marches, "Tramp! Tramp! Tramp!" or "The Prisoners Hope," of the American Civil War in 1864. Root wrote the song to inspire hope in the Union prisoners that help was on its way and that they eventually would be liberated. The march, full of hope and optimism, is thus:

In the prison cell I sit,
Thinking Mother dear, of you,
And our bright and happy home so far away,
And the tears they fill my eyes
Spite of all that I can do,
Tho' I try to cheer my comrades and be gay.
(Chorus)
Tramp, tramp, tramp, the boys are marching,
Cheer up comrades they will come,
And beneath the starry flag
We shall breathe the air again,
Of the freeland in our own beloved home.

The song was also used as a march when the soldiers were marching to the beat of a drum as a morale booster.

"Tramp! Tramp! Tramp!" sheet music cover. Words and music by George F. Root, 1864.

Marching Through Georgia

In 1864, the Union began to consolidate its leadership with President Lincoln appointing General Ulysses S. Grant as Commander-in-Chief of the North with Generals Sherman and Meade commanding the Western and Eastern armies, respectively. With these generals firmly in place, the Union armies began a war of attrition beginning with General William T. Sherman's 100,000-man army that started in Tennessee in May and marched to Atlanta, Georgia, reaching there in early September. The main turning factor in this last stage of the war was General Sherman's successful forty-day siege of Atlanta, which capitulated in mid-November and was nearly burned to the ground. General Sherman then embarked on his famed "March to the Sea," destroying anything useful to the Confederates in his path within a distance of thirty-three miles on both sides of his route. After a 300-mile march from Tennessee through Georgia, Sherman reached the coastal port town of Savannah in December 1864 with a slightly diminished force of 62,000 men. Upon hearing about the deleterious effects of the "March," many Southerners lost their will to continue the struggle. During the month of November, President Lincoln was elected to a second term in office and several songs were written to reflect this fact.

On April 9, 1865, at the Appomattox Court House in Virginia, Confederate General Robert E. Lee, having been encircled after being forced to evacuate the Confederate capital at Richmond, was forced to surrender his Army of Northern Virginia to General Ulysses S. Grant of the Union Army of the Potomac. The surrender officially ended the American Civil War, which lasted almost four years and was the bloodiest war in American history. At the end of the Civil War, to commemorate Sherman's March to the Sea, Henry Clay Work composed a marching song to be accompanied by brass instruments titled "Marching Through Georgia." Obviously the lively melody appealed only to the Union civil war veterans. There were five verses, each adding to the story of the march from start to finish. The first verse and chorus is:

Bring the good old bugle, boys, we'll sing another song
Sing it with a spirit that will start the world along
Sing it as we used to sing it, 50,000 strong
While we were marching through Georgia.
(Chorus)
Hurrah! Hurrah! We bring the jubilee!
Hurrah! Hurrah! The flag that makes you free!
So we sang the chorus from Atlanta to the sea
While we were marching through Georgia.

"For God & Liberty" written to his Excellency, the President of the United States. Sheet music cover. By Harrison Millard, 1864.

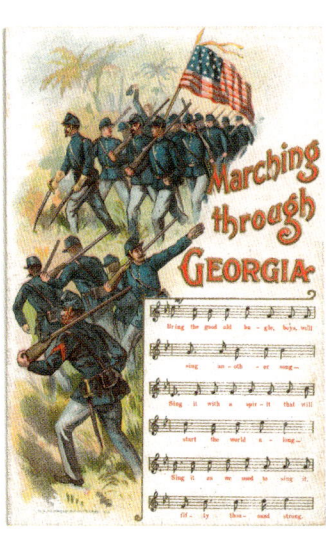

"Marching through Georgia." Published by Chas. Rose; Series 11/18.

"Marching thro' Georgia." Published by L. R. Conwell; Series No. 382.

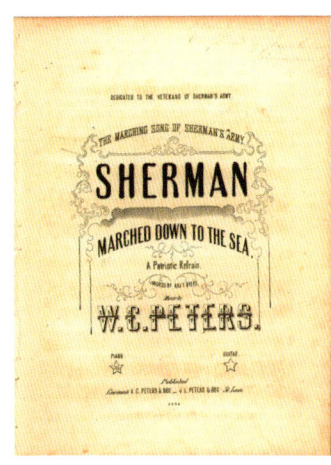

"Sherman Marched Down to the Sea." This marching song was dedicated to the Veterans of Sherman's Army. Words by Adj't Byers; music by W. C Peters. 1865.

"United Confederate Veterans March." Composed by Theo. H. Northrup, 1901.

Thus ends a representation of the most popular songs to come out from the American Civil War. Of all of the American wars to date, the quantity, quality, and variety of the estimated 10,000 songs published has exceeded the output from any of the other conflicts. Two printing inventions that allowed the production and distribution of such a vast quantity of sheet music to music schools, churches, and homes was the lithographic printing process and the high-speed rotary press. Invented in 1796, lithography used a simple chemical process to transfer a drawn image from a smooth surface stone or metal plate to paper. In 1843 to 1847, the rotary press was invented and perfected, which permitted continuous printing from an image etched on a cylinder, thereby allowing the reproduction of low cost copies to number from the hundreds to the thousands. Originally sheet music was tediously engraved using embellished lettering and calligraphic titles without an accompanying image. With inexpensive lithography, an illustrated title page could be included with an image suitable for the music. In approximately the same time frame, the process of chromolithography, patented in 1837, allowed the making of multi-color prints. While printers in the Civil War era utilized some color lithography, much of the mass-produced sheet music was printed on some form of colored paper. In the decades following the Civil War, many veterans groups, such as the Grand Army of the Republic (GAR) from the North and the United Confederate Veterans (UCV) from the South, produced patriotic music as a dedicated remembrance to times past.

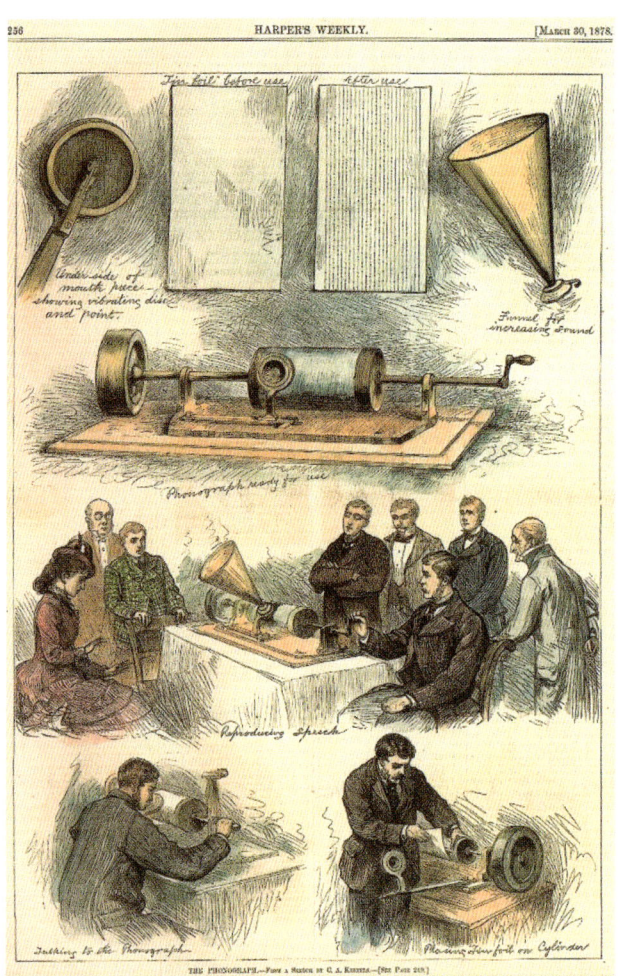

Harper's Weekly, March 30, 1878. Full-page illustration depicting the various steps in producing sound from Edison's phonograph.

In November 1877, twelve years after the end of the American Civil War, a unique patent was given to Thomas Alva Edison for a device to record and reproduce sounds called a phonograph. The first recording medium was a thin sheet of tinfoil but quickly segued to a brown wax cylinder. Edison's cylinder devices were in use until 1912. In 1892, the first firm to play recorded music from flat disks was the Berliner Gramophone. In 1901, the Victor Talking Machine Company was established to play gramophone disk records made out of a hardened rubber compound or a 25% shellac and slate combination. Eventually disk records overtook wax cylinders as the preferred medium. The public, instead of having to travel to a concert hall, church, auditorium or a recital, could now purchase recorded music to enjoy at home with family and friends. With the availability of myriad forms of music, sheet music sales increased as the public wanted to try their hand at playing their own instruments to the music. Typically sheet music was published for the piano in most cases whereas recorded music on cylinders or disks were either classical compositions or some form of patriotic band marches.

The Spanish-American War

In the 1890s, when America was emerging as a world power and, therefore, more aware of their status internationally, events were occurring in the Caribbean that would provoke the country into taking certain aggressive actions based on the Monroe Doctrine. This foreign policy principle, promulgated in 1823 by Secretary of State John Quincy Adams under President James Monroe, stipulated that the United States would not tolerate an European nation attempting to colonize an independent nation in the Americas as well as not to interfere in the affairs of the Western Hemisphere. At this time the fear was that Spain would try to take over its former colonies in South America, which had already declared their independence. However, while the Monroe Doctrine pledged neutrality towards existing European colonies, it advocated liberty for all newly emerging countries of the Americas.

One of the Caribbean colonies of Spain was the island of Cuba. For decades the Cubans tried to resist Spain rule, but were met with crushing defeat. However, word got to the United States concerning alleged atrocities against the Cuban patriots, and American public opinion was aroused against Spain. For that reason the battleship *USS Maine* was sent to the Cuban harbor in Havana in January 1898 to protect American interests during the Cuban revolt. One month later, on February 15, 1898, a mysterious explosion sank the *Maine* causing 261 fatalities out of a complement of 355 men. With the American public enraged — its outrage fostered by evidence of Spanish "brutality" by the competing newspapers of the day — the Administration of President William McKinley was pushed into war with the battle cry of "Remember the Maine" and "To Hell with Spain." On April 25, 1898, the Spanish-American War began with a declaration of war against Spain, backed by the Monroe Doctrine, ostensibly for Cuban independence. The Spanish-American War was fought both in Cuba and in the Spanish colony of the Philippines (for a much longer time). Fourteen weeks later the Spanish sued for peace. As a result of the Treaty of Paris in 1898, the United States temporarily gained control of Cuba and, for $20 million, purchased the Philippines, Puerto Rico, and Guam from Spain. This war produced 332 battle casualties.

"The Spirit of Liberty" song sheet. Marches and Two-Step (no words). Composed by George Rosey; this was written as a result of the Spanish-American War. Original. 1898.

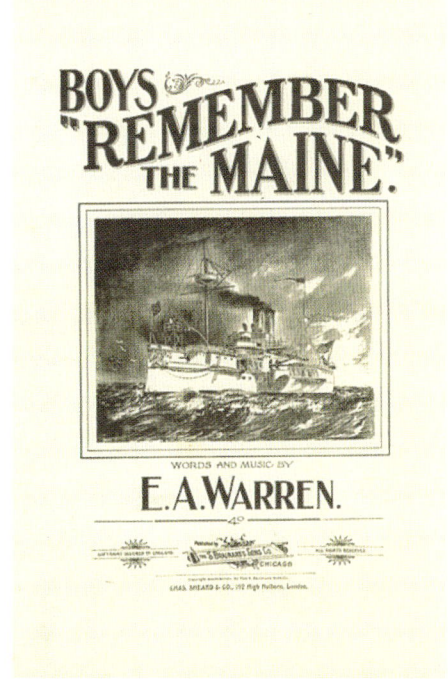

"Boys, Remember the Maine" sheet music cover. Words and music by E. A. Warren. 1898.

"Sinking of the Battleship "Maine" — the prelude to the Spanish American War. Image accompanied Spanish Minister Enrique Duprey DeLome's letter of January 25, 1898, to the Spanish Embassy.

John Philip Sousa

The lead up to and the prosecution of the Spanish-American War during the 1890s produced many patriotic tunes. Originally, popular music was sold primarily as sheet music for playing the piano or small recitals for singing. Now, due to Edison's invention of a phonograph, people could hear reproduced music by many of the popular artists of the day who laboriously recorded music for the "talking machines." One of the most popular musicians/band leaders of that era was John Philip Sousa (1854-1932). Referred to as the "Father of March Music," Sousa was without question the greatest composer of marches (nearly 140) who ever lived. A march is a musical composition utilizing a strong regular rhythm performed by a military band using a combination of drums, woodwinds, and brass in a marching format.

Early in his youth, Sousa showed great musical talent. He became proficient in ten instruments, many of which he learned as an apprentice musician with the United States Marine Corps Band. When he was twenty-six years old, Sousa accepted a position as the leader of the United States Marine Band, which he maintained from 1880 until he resigned in 1892. From the early 1890s until 1917, when he re-enlisted, this time with the Navy, Sousa created and maintained a private band that was in demand everywhere for his patriotic compositions and marches. In 1889, Sousa composed the popular "Washington Post" and "Semper Fidelis," which is the official march of the United States Marine Corps. Charles Burr wrote the lyrics to that march.

However, perhaps Sousa's most famous patriotic march was the "Stars and Stripes Forever," which was first played in Philadelphia on May 14, 1897. It is a tremendously uplifting piece, well-known by all, and played with great gusto complete with crashing cymbals, brass, and piccolos that brings forth a sense of stirring patriotism to everyone who hears it. Because of this sentiment, "Star and Stripes Forever" is, by an Act of Congress, recognized as the National March of the United States of America. Even though Sousa composed many famous marches, the irony is that when Sousa created his own private band (1892-1931) after resigning from the U.S. Marines Band, it was a touring sitting band that played some 15,623 concerts and not one that marched. In forty-one years of the Sousa Band's existence, it only "marched" eight times. Sousa played "The Stars and Stripes Forever" for the last time on the day he died — March 6, 1932. A little-known fact is that Sousa also set his own written lyrics to the music, which consisted of two main verses of eight lines each accompanied by four repeated lines at the end of the verse. A duplicate chorus of nine lines is repeated after each verse. The first verse and chorus follows:

Let martial note in triumph float
And liberty extend its mighty hand
A flag appears 'mid thunderous cheers,
The banner of the Western land.
The emblem of the brave and true
Its folds protect no tyrant crew;
The red and white and starry blue
Is freedom's shield and hope.

Other nations may deem their flags the best
And cheer them with fervid elation
But the flag of the North and South and West
Is the flag of flags, the flag of Freedom's nation.
(Chorus)
Hurrah for the flag of the free!
May it wave as our standard forever,
The gem of the land and of the sea,
The banner of the right.
Let despots remember the day
When our fathers with mighty endeavor
Proclaimed as they marched to the fray
That by their might and by their right
It waves forever.

Composer John Philip Sousa, also known as the "Father of March Music." Portrait by Elmer Chickering, a photographer specializing in portraits in Boston Massachusetts, 1900.

"The Stars and Stripes Forever! March" and "The Stars and Stripes Forever! Song" music sheet covers. Both were by John Philip Sousa. Original. 1897.

President Theodore Roosevelt

During the first decade of the 1900s, the specter of the rise of "Yankee Imperialism" began to raise the hackles of some citizens who were worried that the United States, after obtaining its war spoils from the Spanish-American (and Philippines) War as well as its annexation of the Sandwich (Hawaiian) Islands in 1898, was looking for more territory to acquire. These "isolationists" and anti-imperialists took a backseat to those who were thrilled that the United States was finally taking its rightful place as a world leader. When President McKinley was assassinated in September 1901, Vice President Theodore Roosevelt became President. Teddy Roosevelt was an authentic American hero in that during the Spanish-American War he personally led the 1st U.S. Volunteer Cavalry ("Rough Riders") on a charge to capture San Juan Hill in Cuba on July 1, 1898. When Roosevelt became President, his foreign policies were delineated by the famous slogan: "Speak softly and carry a big stick!" As a result of this quasi-militaristic policy, President Roosevelt made great strides for the completion of the Panama Canal (1904-1914) and sent the "Great White Fleet" (sixteen battleships) from 1907-1909 on a fourteen-month, 43,000-nautical mile voyage around the world to demonstrate "blue water" naval capacity.

Cartoon of Theodore Roosevelt by John T. McCutcheon, an American newspaper political cartoonist for the *Chicago Tribune*, c. early 1900s.

41

"America Forever! March" song sheet (no words). Composed and Published by E. T. Paull. Original. 1898. E. T. Paull (1858-1924) was a composer, music arranger, and sheet music publisher. In order to sell sheet music of songs with little fan base, he printed and marketed uniquely colorful front cover illustrations to catch the eye of buyers. Today original song sheets of Paull's are highly collectible.

The "Rough Riders" were led by Teddy Roosevelt as they fought their way up San Juan Hill, Cuba, July 1, 1898. Postcards publisher unknown.

"The Capture of San Juan Hill." Published by Winsch; Series unknown.

This postcard of the U.S. Battleship *Connecticut* was part of a 24-card series printed of the Great White Fleet by Edward Mitchell. Original photo taken by Enrique Muller.

A real photo postcard of President Roosevelt and Family. Image on postcard by Illustrated Post Card Co.

These alleged jingoistic policies that were set up to demonstrate growing American military might to the world can be personified in this sample of nine sheet music pieces; the titles reflected these outward views backed up by vivid and beautifully rendered artistic chromolithographic patriotic imagery. A very popular song of that era and even today is "Anchors Aweigh." This song was originally written as the fight song of the United States Naval Academy. Over the years various versions of the song's verses and bridge have changed in order to give a broader view of the song, and it has gradually become the song of the U. S. Navy. The phrase "anchor's aweigh" is a report that the anchor has been brought abroad and is clear of the sea bottom. The current song's lyrics include three verses and two bridges of which the second verse is the one most commonly sung:

Anchors Aweigh my boys
Anchors Aweigh
Farewell to foreign shores
We sail at break of day 'ay 'ay 'ay
O'er our last night ashore
Drink to the foam
Until we meet once more
Here's wishing you a happy voyage home!

Illustration of outgoing President Teddy Roosevelt (dressed as a cowboy) handing responsibility (in the form of a baby that looks like Roosevelt labeled "My Policies") to his successor William Howard Taft. Roosevelt's Secretary William Loeb, dressed as a bellboy, carries Roosevelt's "Big Stick." *Puck*, 1909.

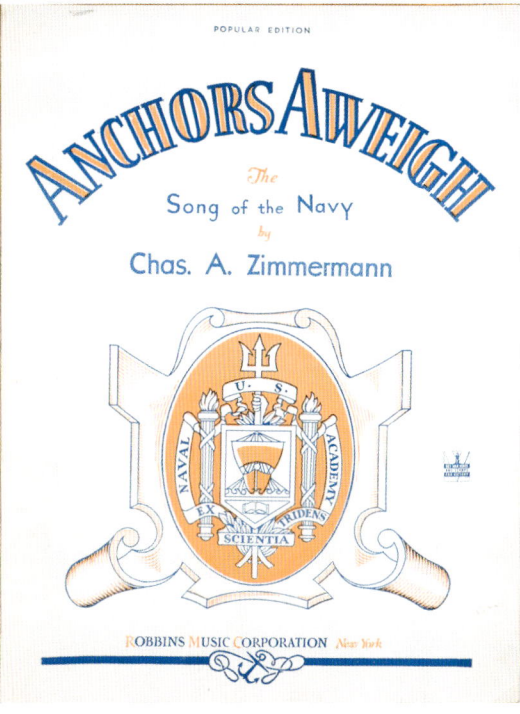

"Anchors Aweigh – The Song of the Navy" song sheet. Written by Chas. A. Zimmerman in 1906; this Lottman/Savino version song sheet is an original from the 1950s.

The most popular patriotic song produced during the first decade of the twentieth century was songwriter George M. Cohan's "You're a Grand Old Flag." Cohan wrote this upbeat patriotic song in 1906 for use in his new musical "George Washington Jr." It quickly became a nationwide sensation and its popularity peaked during America's entry into World War I when it was the first song from a musical to sell more than one million pieces of sheet music. Cohan composed the song made up of two verses and a four-stanza chorus:

Chorus: You're a grand old flag,
You're a high flying flag
And forever in peace may you wave.
You're the emblem of
The land I love.
The home of the free and the brave.
Ev'ry heart beats true.
'neath the Red, White and Blue,
Where there's never a boast or brag.
But should auld acquaintance be forgot,
Keep your eye on the grand old flag.

"You're a Grand Old Flag" sheet music front from 1906. Words and music are by George M. Cohan and were written for his musical "George Washington, Jr." Original new edition from the mid-1930s.

"Uncle Sam's Patrol" song sheet (no words). "A potpourie of popular Patriotic Aires." Composed by John H. Hall. Original. 1904.

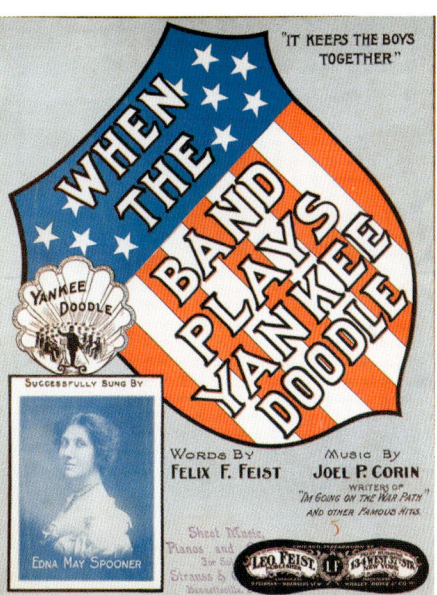
"When the Band Plays Yankee Doodle" song sheet. "When the band plays 'Yankee Doodle' I go fairly off my noodle, And begin to spend my boodle, In a Yankee Doodle way, With three cheers for the Red, White and Blue, For the Army and Navy and You." Words are by Felix F. Feist with music by Joel P. Corin. Original. 1907.

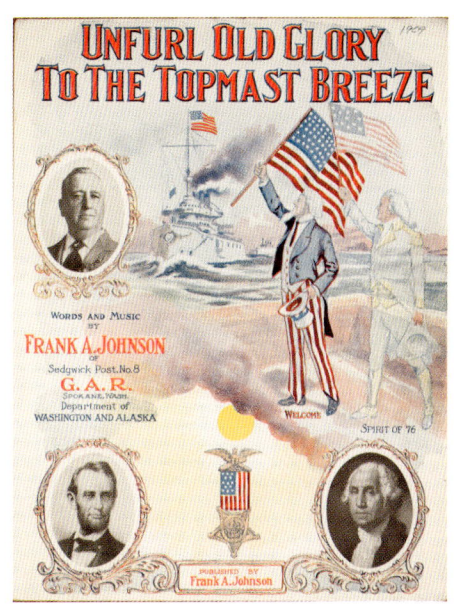
"Unfurl Old Glory to the Top Mast Breeze" song sheet. "Unfurl old glory to the top mast breeze, And show the world the grandest flag on land and on seas, The banner of our liberty Borne bravely thro' the wars, The hope of every free man." Words and music are by Frank A. Johnson. Beautiful front with cameo inserts of Presidents Washington and Lincoln. Original. 1909.

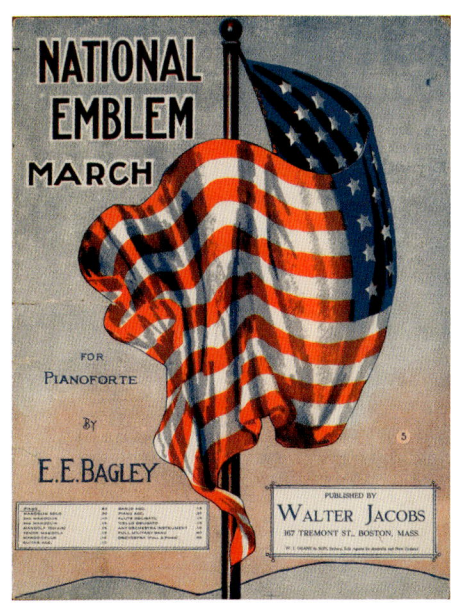
"National Emblem March" song sheet. No words. Composed by E. E. Bagley. Original. 1907.

"Yankee Land" song sheet. March and Two-Step (no words). Composed by Max Hoffmann. Original. 1904.

"Yankiana" song sheet. March and Two-Step (no words). Composed by E. E. Loftis. Original. 1905.

When President Roosevelt decided not to run for President again in 1909, Republican stalwart William Howard Taft defeated Democrat William Jennings Bryan to become the 27th President. He ran for re-election in 1913, but, due to a "Bull Moose" movement orchestrated by former President Roosevelt with the Progressive Party, he lost to Democrat Woodrow Wilson, who campaigned primarily on keeping American neutral in any foreign wars. In the first decade of the twentieth century, America was emerging from the Victorian era with its moralistic sensibilities. A song famous then, while not particularly in the patriotic genre, was a poignant aria composed by Michael W. Balfe from his 1842 operetta, "The Bohemian Girl." The song "Then You'll Remember Me" asked just that in the following decade when our servicemen had to leave their loved ones.

In such a moment I but ask
That you'll remember me
That you'll remember, you'll remember me.

"For President of USA – Wm. H. Taft of Ohio" postcard. Notice the forty-six stars in the flag. Publisher unknown.

"Our Next President" – Wm. H. Taft election postcard. Cameo insert set against the White House. Publisher unknown.

Image of Teddy Roosevelt from the front cover of *Leslie's Illustrated Weekly*, November 9, 1916. Roosevelt is pictured bursting on the scene – on many stages, many platforms. This cartoon caricature appeared two days after the presidential election. Even though Roosevelt was not a candidate in the election, he was a preeminent figure on the national scene.

Cartoon illustration depicting the new President William Taft and his uncertain relationship with the GOP (Republican) and Teddy Roosevelt. Due to a third party "Bull Moose" campaign led by Roosevelt, Taft lost to Wilson in the 1913 election.

"You'll Remember Me." A song written about soldiers leaving for duty hoping to be remembered. Postcard published by GDD, Series 2032.

World War I Era Music

President Wilson's first term (1913-1917) was marked by "progressive" legislation including establishing the Federal Reserve, instigating a federal income tax, and providing much support for the growing women's suffrage movement. On July 28, 1914, World War I started between the Entente (Allies) and the Central Powers (Germany/Italy/Turkey). During his first term, Wilson proclaimed America's neutrality as U. S. intervention was very unpopular with the citizens. Democratically-aligned newspapers and even sheet music reflected the general population's view of pacifism or isolationism with a patriotic bent.

"Don't Take my Darling Boy Away" song sheet. Words are by Will Dillon and the music is by Albert von Tilzer. "No, Captain please, Here on my knees, I plead for one I adore." Anti-war theme. Original. 1915.

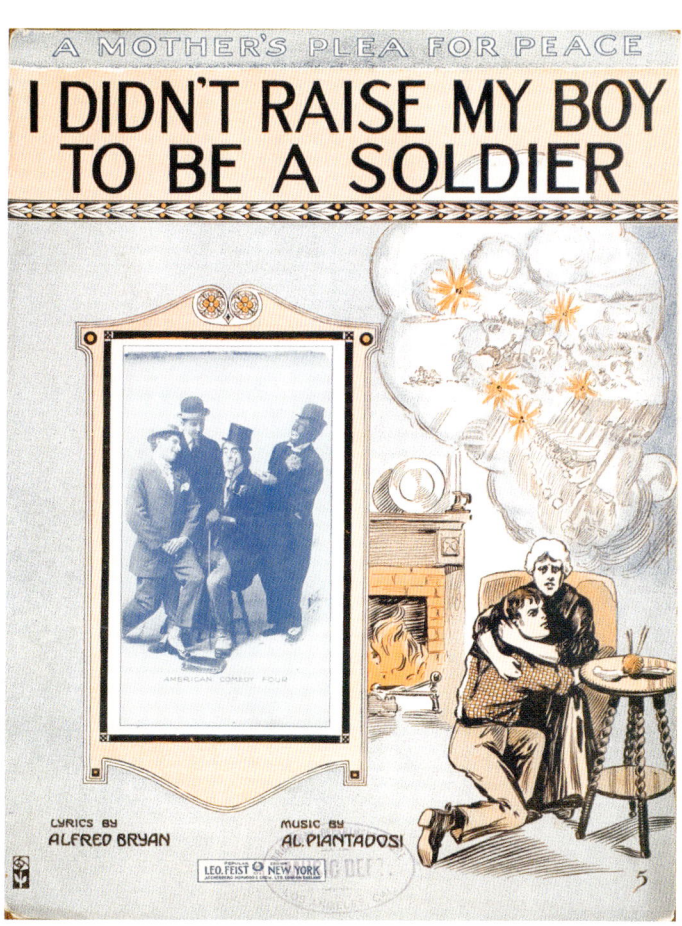

"I Didn't Raise my Son to be a Soldier" song sheet. A mother pleas for peace in this anti-war theme. Lyrics are by Alfred Bryan with music by Alfred Piantadosi. "…I brought him up to be my pride and joy, Who dares to place a musket on his shoulder, To shoot some other mother's darling boy?" Original. 1915.

"L-I-B-E-R-T-Y – The Song of Our Land" song sheet. Composed by Ted S. Barron. "At a grand old meeting on Decoration Day, There spoke a veteran old and gray…" Original. 1916.

Wilson's slogan for his re-election campaign for a second term was "He kept us out of war!" Unfortunately that was not to be. On January 9, 1917, Germany announced unrestricted submarine warfare on all shipping from America to Europe. Also, the famous "Zimmerman Telegram" sent from Germany to Mexico pledging help for Mexico to recapture its territories lost to the United States due to the Mexican-American War of 1848 if they joined in the fight against the United States was made public on March 1, 1917. With these two situations pending, Wilson had no choice but to ask Congress to declare war on the Central Powers on April 2, 1917. He declared that "armed neutrality" was no longer an option. Wilson concluded with the statement that the "world must be again safe for democracy." Congress passed Wilson's request on April 4, 1917. Prior to this declaration, there was much anti-war sentiment and the "saber-rattling" to help the Allies with their war effort made many citizens uncomfortable. The new Selective Service Act of 1917 conscription, or draft of all able-bodied men ages 18 to 45, meant that many loved ones would be called to fight in another foreign war. Anti-war sentiment soon evaporated and, with America firmly on the side of the Triple Entente (Allied Powers), there was a demonstrated effort to purge the world of the hated German Kaiser.

Over There

Out of the thousands of songs that were written expressly for events leading up to and including America's involvement in World War I, the most popular one was George M. Cohan's "Over There." This song had a long reach as it was also very popular during the initial stages of World War II as well as being one of the main songs in a very popular musical in 1942. From the lyrics of this song came the famous slogan: "The Yanks are coming!" Cohan penned two verses that included a rousing chorus:

Over there, over there,
Send the word, send the word over there
That the Yanks are coming, the Yanks are coming
The drums rum-tumming everywhere.
So prepare, say a prayer,
Send the word, send the word to beware
We'll be over, we're coming over,
And we won't come back till it's over, over there.

President Wilson described "Over There" (the full title was "Your Song – My Song – Our Boys' Song! Over There) as "a genuine inspiration to all American manhood." The graphics of the sheet music shown here is based on illustrator Norman Rockwell's painting for *LIFE Magazine* in 1918.

"America's Greatest March" song sheet (no words). March composed by David H. Hawthorne. The front cover has cameos of Presidents Woodrow Wilson, Washington, and Lincoln. Original. 1917.

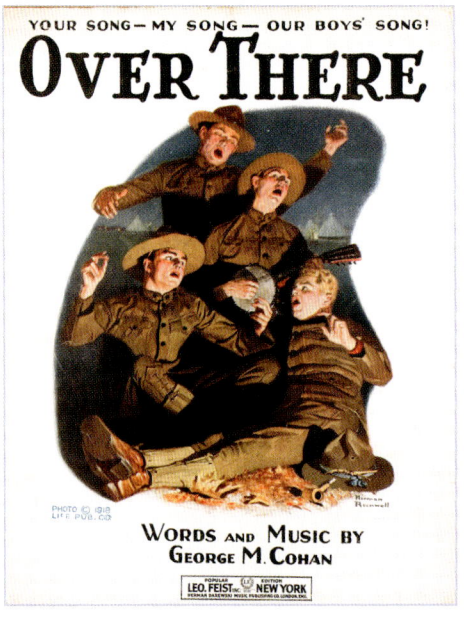

"Over There: Your Song – My Song – Our Boys' Song!" song sheet. Words and music are by George M. Cohan. The front cover graphics were drawn by Norman Rockwell and appeared on a *LIFE* cover in 1918. Original. 1917.

Other Wartime Music

The majority of the patriotic sheet music published during 1917 had to do with exhortations to enlist (see Uncle Sam chapter), training camp life, saying goodbye as the troops were leaving, and the enthusiasm that victory would be theirs although the road ahead would be hard. Unfortunately none of the American soldiers called to arms would be taking the road less traveled!

The first U.S. American Expeditionary Forces (AEF), under the leadership of Major General John J. "Black Jack" Pershing, reached France on May 3, 1917. Within one year, more than one million troops were stationed in France, of which one-half were stationed on the front lines. The first four combat-ready divisions were deployed with French and British forces to gain some combat experience; the first offensive action and victory for the AEF (28th Infantry Regiment of the US First Division) was on May 28, 1918, at the Battle of Cantigny with some French forces. By May 30th, the battle area was secured with the 28th Regiment suffering 1,067 casualties (killed, wounded, and missing). It was America's initial commitment in blood for democracy in France. By September 1918, General Pershing was in command of the American First Army of 500,000 men, which fought in the battles of the Saint-Mihiel salient as well as the Meuse-Argonne offensive that employed more than one million American and French troops. By the time the Armistice was signed, stopping all combat operations at the eleventh hour of the eleventh day of the eleventh month (November 11, 1918), most of the AEF, including air support, were worthy battle-hardened veterans. In a relatively short period of time (5-1/2 months), the AEF experienced 116,708 casualties (53,600 KIA) and 205,700 wounded. It took six more months to conclude the peace negotiations with the Treaty of Versailles signed on June 28, 1919, (five years to the day WW I began) between Germany and the three principal Allied Powers, thus officially ending "the war to end all wars." The Soviet Union concluded its own treaty with Germany in 1922.

Since the actual combat that the AEF experienced was of short duration, sheet music pieces were illustrative of the positive looking themes that surrounded America's involvement in, as it was then called, The Great War. The first two pieces "Keep the Trench Fires Burning" and "Somewhere in France is Daddy" are poignantly edgier and contrapuntal to Cohan's optimistic "Over There." The titles of the final four pieces were expressions of optimism that the troops would defeat Germany and then come home, the job being accomplished, to a great measure of gratitude and thanks from America.

In summary, sheet music of the 1916-1919 era portrayed both pacifist and patriotic sentiments. Once war was declared, there was an enormous amount of patriotic sheet music published in very vivid imagery in colors of red, white, and blue. Also if sheet music is arranged in some chronological order, they can tell a story of the war's progress through various music titles, images, and sentiments. Many of the titles seemed optimistic based on the original Allied war goal to invade and subjugate Germany and, while that main goal was not accomplished, leading to an even greater war just twenty-one years later, the world was at peace. Probably the most famous song that was written during the last year of the war in 1918 was Irving Berlin's "God Bless America," but that song was not greatly popular; the lyrics were more in the form of a prayer whereas the patriotic songs of that era were more robust.

"What Kind of American are You?" song sheet. Words are by Lew Brown and Chas. McCarron and music by Albert von Tilzer. A decidedly pro-war theme with an angry Uncle Sam asking: "What are you doing over here? It's time to show what you intend to do. If they tramp old Glory will you think that they are right, Or will you stand behind your land and fight with all your might?" Original. 1917.

"The Minute Men of To-Day are Going to Plattsburg" sheet music cover. Plattsburg, New York, was a famous training camp for soldiers before embarking overseas. 1917.

This real photo postcard (RPPC) of a World War I American typical "doughboy."

"We're Going Over" song sheet. Composed by Andrew B. Sterling, Bernie Grossman, and Arthur Lange. "We're going over, we're going over, They want us to settle that fuss, and they put it up to us, So what do we care, so what do we care…" Original. 1917.

"Au Revoir, But Not Good-Bye (Soldier Boy)" song sheet. Words by Lew Brown and music by Albert von Tilzer: "Au Revoir not Goodbye, Soldier boy. Brush that tear drop from your eye, Soldier boy. When you're on the deep blue sea, Will you sometimes think of me? I'll be waiting anxiously, Soldier boy." Original. 1917.

"When Yankee Doodle Learns to Parlez Vous Francais" song sheet. Words are by Will Hart and music by Ed Nelson: "When Yankee Doodle learns to Parlez vous Francais, Parlez vous Francais, in the proper way, He will call each girlie "Ma Cherie," to every Miss that wants a kiss he'll say Wee, Wee…" Original. 1917.

"It's A Long Way to Berlin, But We'll Get There" song sheet. Words are by Arthur Fields and music by Leon Flatow: "It's a long way to Berlin, but we'll get there. Uncle Sam will show the way, Over the line, then across the Rhine, Shouting Hip! Hip! Hooray!" Original. 1917.

Souvenir postcard fold-out of Camp Mills, New York. Postmarked September 8, 1918, it was sent by a trainee from Company K, 343rd Infantry. Front and back covers are each bordered by different scenes of all matters of military operations. The sequences of the images of the soldiers are as follows: "On the hike" and "digging trenches;" "Roll call" and "shelter tent inspection;" "Squad drill" and "practice march."

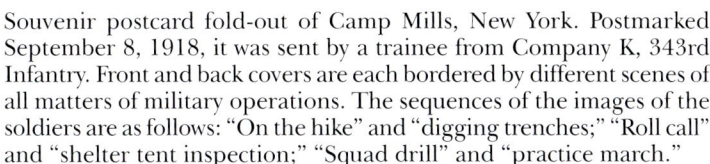

51

"Just Like Washington Crossed the Delaware, General Pershing will Cross the Rhine" song sheet. Words are by Howard Johnson and music by Geo. W. Meyer. Front sheet cover has a cameo of General Pershing. "Just like Washington crossed the Delaware, so will Pershing cross the Rhine, as they followed after George, at dear old Valley Forge, our boys will break that line. It's for your land and my land and the sake of Auld Lang Syne." Original. 1918.

"When I Send You A Picture Of Berlin" song sheet. Composed by Frank Fay, Ben Ryan, and Dave Dreyer. "But when I send you a picture of Berlin you'll know it's over, 'Over There' then I'm coming home." Original. 1918.

"Good-Bye Germany" song sheet. Composed by J. Edwin McConnell and Lincoln McConnell. "Goodbye Germany so long Germany You've brought the eagle down on your head– For you've riled old Uncle Sam and the people of his land. When Uncle Sam goes after you the whole big world knows that you are thru So goodbye Germany!" Original. 1918.

"Welcome Home" song sheet. Words are by Bud Green and music by Ed Nelson. "Skies of gray have given way to brightness, Hearts that once were sad are feeling gay, The news has flashed around, Our boys are homeward bound and we will be there to say…Welcome Home!" Original. 1918.

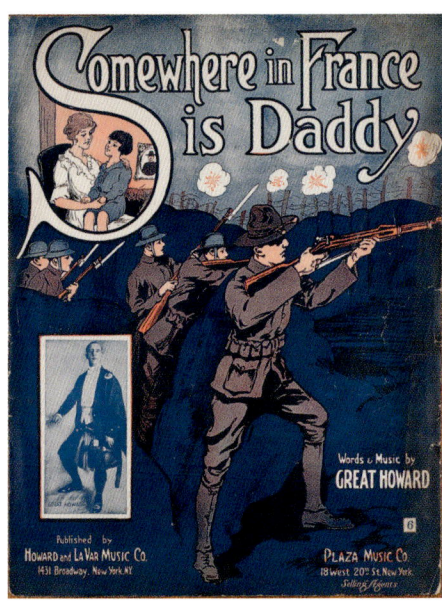  

"Somewhere in France is Daddy" song sheet. Words and music by Great Howard: "Somewhere in France is Daddy, Somewhere in France is he. Fighting for home and country, Fighting my lad, for Liberty. I pray every night for the Allies and ask God to help them win, For our Daddy won't come back 'till the Stars and Stripes they'll tack on Kaiser William's flag staff in Berlin." Original. 1918.

"Keep the Trench Fires Going for the Boys Out There" song sheet. Words are by Eddie Moran and music by Harry von Tilzer. "Keep the Trench fires going for the boys out there, Let's play fair, do our share for boys are fighting for you and me-can't you see? For you and me and Liberty." Original. 1918.

Image honoring ARMISTICE DAY, November 11. Reproduced from U.S. Flags Store. Publisher and date unknown.

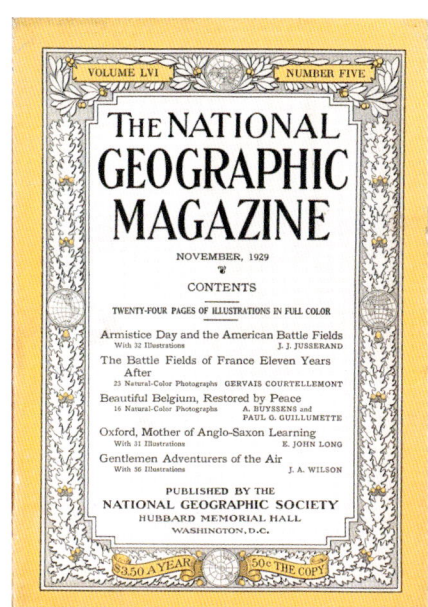

VOLUME LVI NUMBER FIVE

THE NATIONAL GEOGRAPHIC MAGAZINE

NOVEMBER, 1929

CONTENTS

TWENTY-FOUR PAGES OF ILLUSTRATIONS IN FULL COLOR

Armistice Day and the American Battle Fields
With 32 Illustrations J. J. JUSSERAND

The Battle Fields of France Eleven Years After
25 Natural-Color Photographs GERVAIS COURTELLEMONT

Beautiful Belgium, Restored by Peace
16 Natural-Color Photographs A. BUYSSENS and PAUL G. GUILLUMETTE

Oxford, Mother of Anglo-Saxon Learning
With 31 Illustrations E. JOHN LONG

Gentlemen Adventurers of the Air
With 56 Illustrations J. A. WILSON

PUBLISHED BY THE
NATIONAL GEOGRAPHIC SOCIETY
HUBBARD MEMORIAL HALL
WASHINGTON, D.C.

$3.50 A YEAR 50c THE COPY

The National Geographic Magazine featuring article "Armistice Day and American Battle Fields," November 1929.

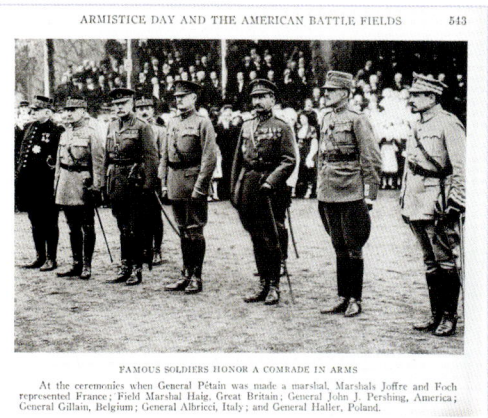

ARMISTICE DAY AND THE AMERICAN BATTLE FIELDS 543

FAMOUS SOLDIERS HONOR A COMRADE IN ARMS

At the ceremonies when General Pétain was made a marshal, Marshals Joffre and Foch represented France; Field Marshal Haig, Great Britain; General John J. Pershing, America; General Gillain, Belgium; General Albricci, Italy; and General Haller, Poland.

"Famous Soldiers Honor A Comrade In Arms" during Armistice celebrations. Seven famous generals of the Triple Entente Powers gather to honor Marshall Petain of France.

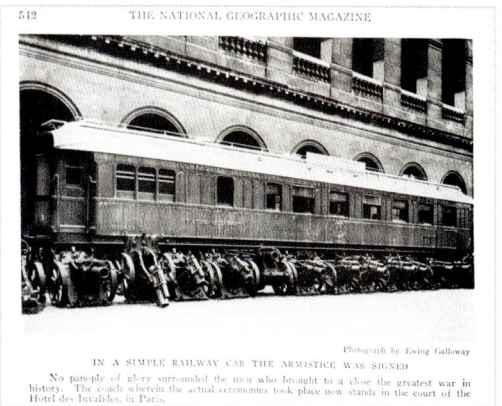

542 THE NATIONAL GEOGRAPHIC MAGAZINE

Photograph by Ewing Galloway

IN A SIMPLE RAILWAY CAR THE ARMISTICE WAS SIGNED

No panoply of glory surrounded the men who brought to a close the greatest war in history. The coach wherein the actual ceremonies took place now stands in the court of the Hôtel des Invalides, in Paris.

"In a simple railway car the Armistice was signed" on November 11, 1918, at 5 a.m., with hostilities to end six hours later at 11 a.m. The railway car was located in the Forest of Compiegne, thirty-nine miles north of Paris, France.

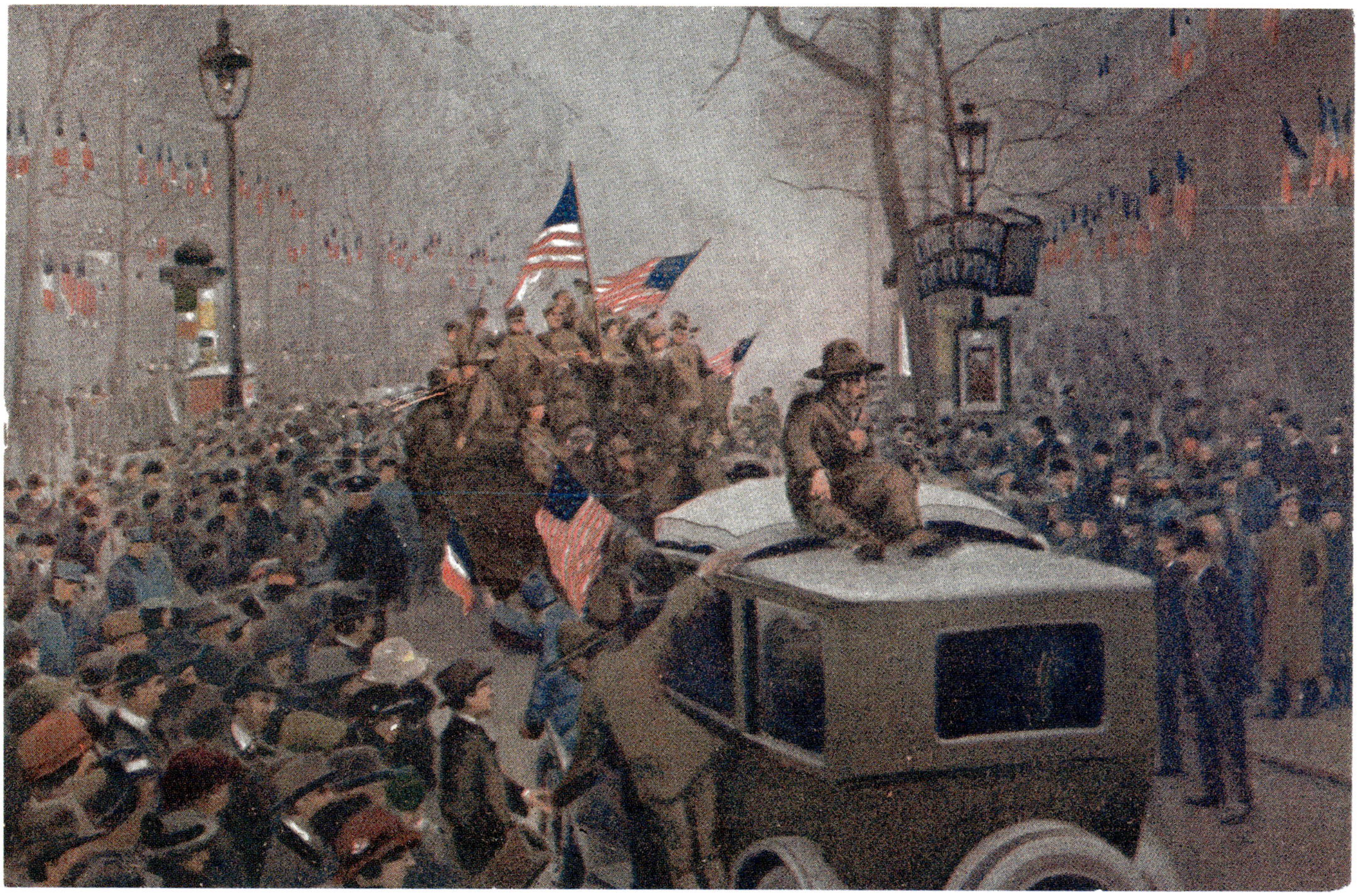

Fanciful image of an Armistice Day celebration in New York City, a joyous occasion.
Postcard. Editions d'Art Yvon Paris, France. American Legion.

Post-World War I Life

After World War I came to an end, American patriotism hit a low point as there were seemingly little external threats to the nation during the "Roaring Twenties" and into the "Depression" of the 1930s. A more subtle threat, however, was the emergence of Soviet Communism and the birth of several radical political parties that advocated a change in America's democratic form of governance. Two long-evolving political movements resulted in amendments to the Constitution. On October 28, 1919, the 18th Amendment to the United States Constitution was passed (National Prohibition or Volstead Act) prohibiting the production, sale, and transport of intoxicating beverages. It was eventually repealed by the 21st Amendment in December 1933. Of equally long stature was the Women's Suffrage Movement, whose long-term aim was the empowerment of women to vote, which culminated in the passing of the 19th Amendment on August 18, 1920, prohibiting the denial of vote based on gender. The emancipation of women after this amendment was accepted with mixed views until the coming war years.

During the 1920s, a new form of entertainment format was introduced: wireless telegraphy or, as it's commonly known, the radio. The first radio news program aired on August 31, 1920. The first regular entertainment programs were broadcast in 1922 and, within ten years, the "Golden Age" of radio was thrust upon the American public by broadcasting in every feasible form of genre and entertainment format available. As most of the early radio was music format programming, the fear was that sheet music sales would plummet as everyone could listen to "free" radio. While sheet music sales did dip for awhile, radio brought to the home a wide range of music from classical and jazz to Big Bands and country. In most cases many of the tunes could be played at home on the piano so sheet music sales made a rebound.

Program directors of embryonic radio stations, in order to survive competition for advertised dollars, had to have some way to calculate the popularity of broadcast music. *Billboard* magazine came to the rescue. Founded in 1894, *Billboard* is one of the oldest trade publications in the world. With the advent of radio, *Billboard* began covering radio music programming. With the development of the coin-operated jukebox industry in the 1930s, *Billboard* began publishing hit parade music charts in 1936 based on popularity of record sales, jukebox usage, and radio airplay. Sheet music sales closely reflected the popular tunes spread over three genre-specific charts: Pop, Rhythm and Blues, and Country and Western.

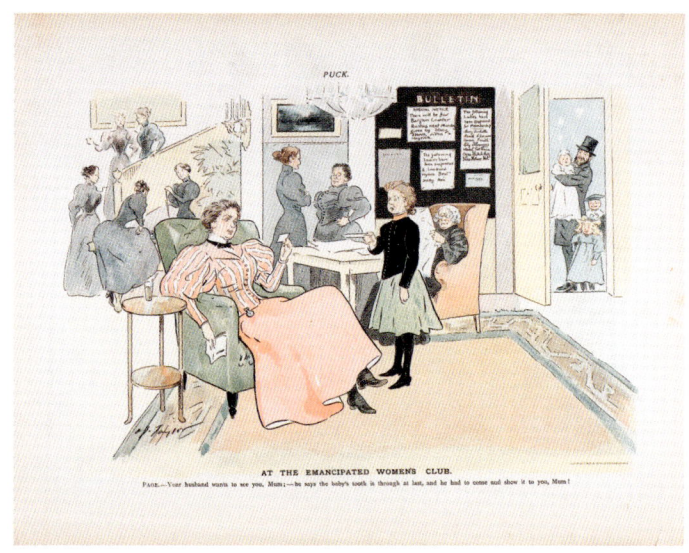

Political cartoon appearing in *Puck*, October, 1920: As the result of women's suffrage, women now have an equal place in society (or perhaps more!).

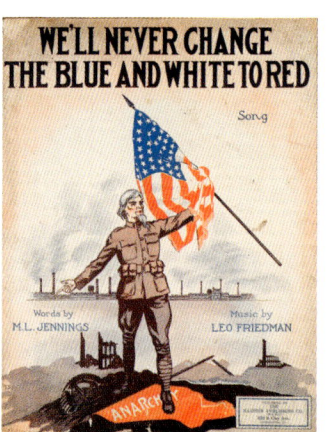

"We'll Never Change the Blue and White to Red" song sheet. Words are by M. L. Jennings and music by Leo Friedman: An anti-Communist song featuring a graphic image of Uncle Sam in uniform holding an American flag over the ruins of anarchy. "Then let us stand by old Red, White and Blue! To victory she has always led, beneath her folds is writ a story true; We'll never change the Blue and White to red." Original. 1919.

Political Cartoon: "If You are Good enough for War You are Good enough to Vote" — a plea for women's suffrage. An iconic image of Uncle Sam as Public Opinion embracing a Nurse as American Womanhood. Artist: Morris. 1919.

"Famous Soldiers Honor A Comrade In Arms" during Armistice celebrations. Seven famous generals of the Triple Entente Powers gather to honor Marshall Petain of France.

The National Geographic Magazine featuring article "Armistice Day and American Battle Fields," November 1929.

"In a simple railway car the Armistice was signed" on November 11, 1918, at 5 a.m., with hostilities to end six hours later at 11 a.m. The railway car was located in the Forest of Compiegne, thirty-nine miles north of Paris, France.

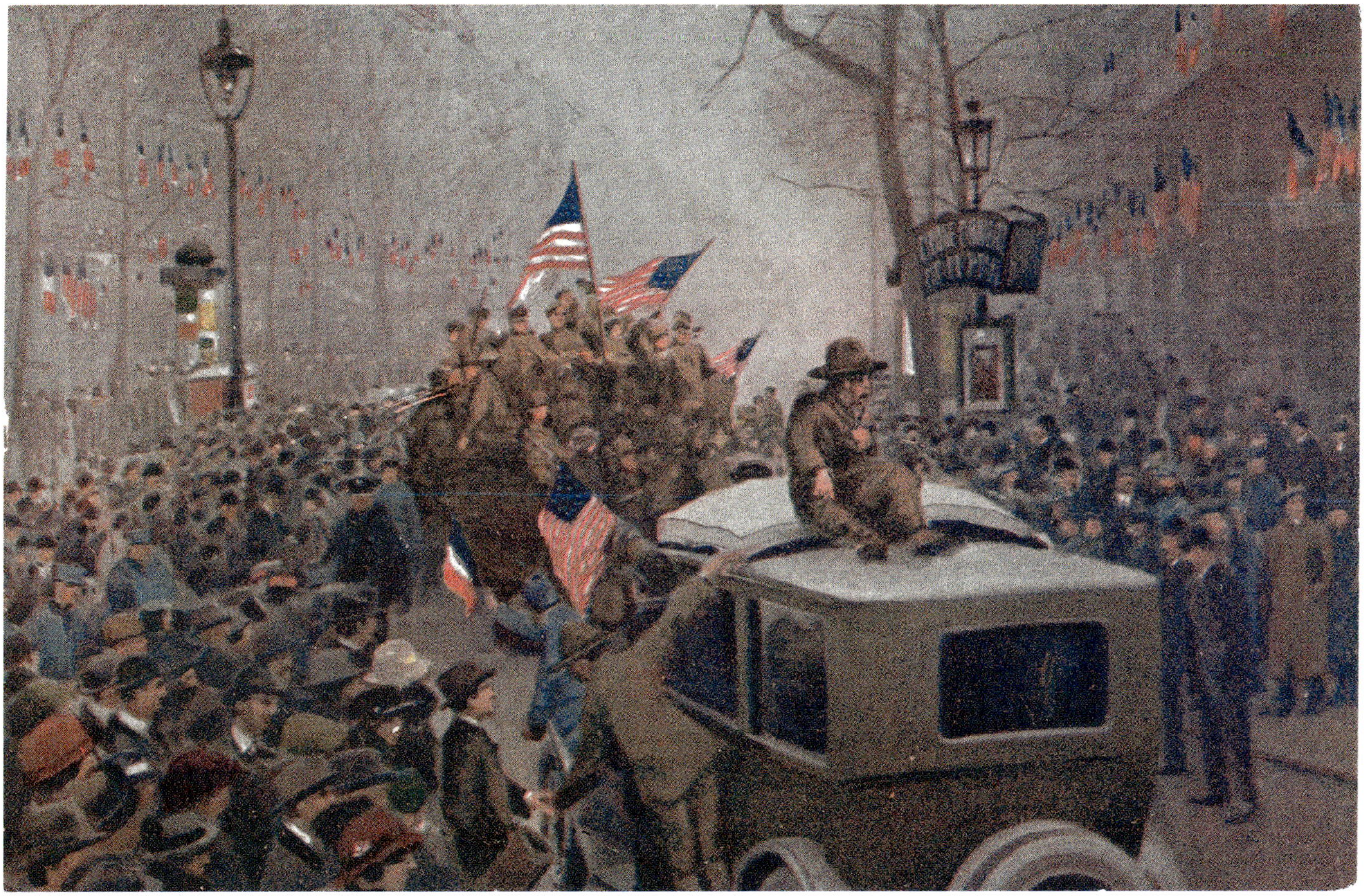

Fanciful image of an Armistice Day celebration in New York City, a joyous occasion.
Postcard. Editions d'Art Yvon Paris, France. American Legion.

Post-World War I Life

After World War I came to an end, American patriotism hit a low point as there were seemingly little external threats to the nation during the "Roaring Twenties" and into the "Depression" of the 1930s. A more subtle threat, however, was the emergence of Soviet Communism and the birth of several radical political parties that advocated a change in America's democratic form of governance. Two long-evolving political movements resulted in amendments to the Constitution. On October 28, 1919, the 18th Amendment to the United States Constitution was passed (National Prohibition or Volstead Act) prohibiting the production, sale, and transport of intoxicating beverages. It was eventually repealed by the 21st Amendment in December 1933. Of equally long stature was the Women's Suffrage Movement, whose long-term aim was the empowerment of women to vote, which culminated in the passing of the 19th Amendment on August 18, 1920, prohibiting the denial of vote based on gender. The emancipation of women after this amendment was accepted with mixed views until the coming war years.

During the 1920s, a new form of entertainment format was introduced: wireless telegraphy or, as it's commonly known, the radio. The first radio news program aired on August 31, 1920. The first regular entertainment programs were broadcast in 1922 and, within ten years, the "Golden Age" of radio was thrust upon the American public by broadcasting in every feasible form of genre and entertainment format available. As most of the early radio was music format programming, the fear was that sheet music sales would plummet as everyone could listen to "free" radio. While sheet music sales did dip for awhile, radio brought to the home a wide range of music from classical and jazz to Big Bands and country. In most cases many of the tunes could be played at home on the piano so sheet music sales made a rebound.

Program directors of embryonic radio stations, in order to survive competition for advertised dollars, had to have some way to calculate the popularity of broadcast music. *Billboard* magazine came to the rescue. Founded in 1894, *Billboard* is one of the oldest trade publications in the world. With the advent of radio, *Billboard* began covering radio music programming. With the development of the coin-operated jukebox industry in the 1930s, *Billboard* began publishing hit parade music charts in 1936 based on popularity of record sales, jukebox usage, and radio airplay. Sheet music sales closely reflected the popular tunes spread over three genre-specific charts: Pop, Rhythm and Blues, and Country and Western.

Political cartoon appearing in *Puck*, October, 1920: As the result of women's suffrage, women now have an equal place in society (or perhaps more!).

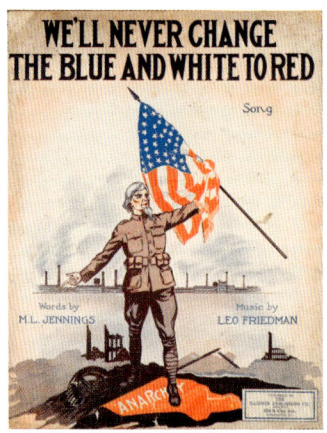

"We'll Never Change the Blue and White to Red" song sheet. Words are by M. L. Jennings and music by Leo Friedman: An anti-Communist song featuring a graphic image of Uncle Sam in uniform holding an American flag over the ruins of anarchy. "Then let us stand by old Red, White and Blue! To victory she has always led, beneath her folds is writ a story true; We'll never change the Blue and White to red." Original. 1919.

Political Cartoon: "If You are Good enough for War You are Good enough to Vote" — a plea for women's suffrage. An iconic image of Uncle Sam as Public Opinion embracing a Nurse as American Womanhood. Artist: Morris. 1919.

"Uncle Sam, Suffragee" Uncle Sam decked out as a suffragette in support of women's suffrage. Publisher is unknown; "Suffragette" Series No. 6.

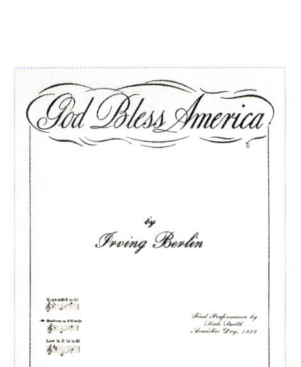

"Did I Save My Country for this!" exclaims George Washington to the ladies of the Suffrage movement. Postcard: Artist signed HBG (HB Griggs). Published by L & E; Series No. 2268.

"God Bless America" song sheet. Composed by Irving Berlin (in 1906), it was rewritten in 1938. First introduced and performed by Kate Smith, Armistice Day, 1938. Original. 1938.

God Bless America

From the mid-1930s, there were worldwide concerns about the emerging militaristic aggressiveness of what would come to be known as the Axis Powers (i.e. Germany and Japan). As the United States was still in the late throes of the economic Depression, American citizens' concerns were of an internal nature rather than external. However, the now very famous songwriter, Irving Berlin, dusted off his original "God Bless America," first written in 1906 in a vastly different era, and revised some of the words in the song to reflect these growing concerns of malevolent dictatorships on the rise. The revised song was introduced by Kathryn (Kate) Smith, the inspirational songstress, on Armistice Day 1938 on her radio variety show. While "God Bless America" contains dramatic words and melody, no singer except Kate Smith, with her strong voice, could truly do the song justice especially with her arrangement accompanied by a full orchestra and chorus in a grand march tempo. The two traditional stanzas are:

While the storm clouds gather far across the sea,
Let us swear allegiance to a land that's free,
Let us all be grateful for a land so fair,
As we raise our voices in a solemn prayer.
God bless America,
Land that I love.
Stand beside her, and guide her
Through the night with a light from above.
From the mountains, to the prairies,
To the oceans, white with foam
God bless America, My home sweet home
God bless America, My home sweet home.

The first stanza is not performed very often as it reflected Irving Berlin's fears of the emergence of Nazi Germany. However, since 9/11, at many professional baseball games, during the seventh-inning stretch "God bless America" has now been substituted for "Take Me Out to the Ballgame." Each major league baseball team has a choice in the matter of substitution.

Pearl Harbor

The fears of another war came true, this time World War II, when Germany attacked Poland on September 1, 1939, eliciting declarations of war on Germany by France, Great Britain, and most of their Commonwealth countries. Unlike World War I, Germany was able to conquer and control much of continental Europe in short order. America tried to stay neutral, but that fanciful idea was crushed when the Japanese Empire attacked the United States territory of the Hawaiian Islands as well as European possessions in South East Asia and the Pacific Ocean. In a famous speech to the Joint Session of Congress requesting a declaration of war, President Franklin Delano Roosevelt emotionally said: "Yesterday, December 7, 1941…a day which will live in infamy…" This address has been considered as one of the great political speeches of the twentieth century. Upon this speech Congress passed a formal declaration of war with Japan on December 8th. Patriotic slogans such as "Remember Pearl Harbor" and "Remember December 7th" were adopted as rallying cries to avenge Pearl Harbor.

An iconic view looking northwest toward "Battleship Row" located near Ford Island Naval Air Station. Of the seven battleships moored at the east side of Ford Island, four were sunk and one suffered heavy damage. In this view the *USS California* (left front) was torpedoed twice while most of the billowing smoke is coming from the doomed *USS Arizona*. On December 7, 1941, the sneak attack by the Japanese naval forces forced President Roosevelt to ask Congress to declare war on Japan. *Official U. S. Navy Photograph 1941 courtesy of Naval History and Heritage Collection (NHHC).*

Pearl Harbor
"A Date Which Will Live In Infamy"

The USS Arizona burns and sinks after a direct hit by a Japanese 1,760-pound, armor-piercing bomb penetrated the top deck of her forward magazine, resulting in the leaning of the foremast due to the collapse of the superstructure. Approximately 1,177 officers and crew of the USS Arizona were killed, representing forty-nine percent of the total killed throughout all of the Pearl Harbor attack. Official U. S. Navy Photograph 1941 courtesy of Naval History and Heritage Collection (NHHC).

The Japanese attack at Pearl Harbor, December 7, 1941, was responsible for a "catch word" song: "Praise the Lord and Pass the Ammunition." Probably the first patriotic song that was written during the very early stages of World War II, "Praise the Lord…" was based on an actual incident that was popularized by the press. Contrary to the sheet music imagery that shows a land-based gunnery crew firing at and being attacked by a Japanese Zero airplane, the true story is different. During the Pearl Harbor attack, Chaplain Howell Forgy was stationed aboard the USS New Orleans. During a point when the USS New Orleans was under air attack, the ship's electrical power failed; ammunition had to be manually lifted up through several decks to the guns aloft. Since this was a strenuous job under horrific battle conditions, the good Chaplain took it upon himself to walk along the line of men who were risking their lives to compliment and cheer them on by uttering that now famous line. This incident was verified to the press, which needed some good news from the attack on Pearl Harbor to share with the American people. From that, a patriotic song of the same title was written by Frank Loesser in 1942 and remained popular for several years.

This poster depicts the bombing of the USS Arizona during the attack on Pearl Harbor. Courtesy of Douglas Sterner-Webmaster for Home of Heroes (www.homeofheroes.com).

"Praise the Lord and Pass the Ammunition!!" song sheet. Written after the Pearl Harbor attack, the words and music are by Frank Loesser. "Praise the Lord, we're on a mighty mission! All aboard! We're not a goin' fishin', Praise the Lord and pass the ammunition and we'll all stay free." Original. 1942.

World War II

When the United States Congress declared war on Japan on December 8, 1941, Germany then declared war on the United States on December 11, 1941, thus thrusting America into another unwanted world war. As providence would have it, there was already in place from World War I a peacetime draft mechanism, which was codified into the Selective Training and Service Act of 1940. The STSA in 1941, working through the Selective Service System, initiated the first peacetime conscription or draft for men aged 18 to 45 with a possible service requirement of eighteen months. Due to the onslaught of World War II, America initiated a massive draft that registered 50 million men, of which 36 million were classified and 10 million inducted for the length of the war plus six months.

When America's involvement in World War II began, the radio was the single largest communication format per household, even exceeding the telephone. Although only fifteen years old at the beginning of the war, AM radio coverage exceeded 95% in most urban centers of the country. News, weather, crop reports, variety shows, soap operas, and music permeated available households. Therefore, it was now possible to transmit the latest popular patriotic-style songs to the Armed Forces through Armed Forces Radio and to the civilian population through a host of AM stations.

Unlike the more aggressive songs that expressed contempt and scorn for Germany and its leader Kaiser Wilhelm during World War I, the songs produced during World War II generally had a much softer message of hope, peace, and even some comedy. Songs like "When The Lights Go On Again (All Over The World)," "You'd Be So Nice To Come Home To," "I'll Be Seeing You," "Boogie Boogie Bugle Boy," and the comedic "Der Fuehrer's Face" by Spike Jones set the tone for most quasi-patriotic renderings. However, some songs such as "I Am An American!" was unabashedly patriotic in tone while other songs were in the form of requests such as "Any Bonds Today?" In these two cases the patriotic images of Uncle Sam were used to spur sales. Likewise song books such as "American Patriotic Songs" were produced during this time enabling the user to master any number of newly written patriotic songs as well as old favorites from many wars past.

Some of the best music to emerge from World War II was in the form of songs written for Broadway musicals and motion pictures. In 1942, Irving Berlin, with the permission of the Army, wrote a wartime musical and composed much of the lyrics for "This Is the Army." Songs such as "This Is the Army Mr. Jones," "I'm Getting Tired So I Can Sleep," and "I Left My Heart at the Stage Door Canteen" were very popular and entered into wartime vernacular. The stage play premiered on Broadway on Independence Day 1942, and ran until September 26, 1942. The play was such a success that it took to the road with an all (integrated) soldier cast on a national tour and earned more than $2 million for the Army Emergency Relief Fund.

In order to reach a larger segment of the American population, a wartime movie picture of the same name, designed to boost wartime morale, was made by Warner Brothers and released August 14, 1943. This film featured nineteen songs composed by Irving Berlin, who, in the movie, sang his own "Oh! How I Hate To Get Up In The Morning." One of the starring actors was Lt. Ronald Reagan, who would later become the 40th President of the United States and serve two terms (1981-1989). Kate Smith also made an appearance, singing "God Bless America," which was also written by Irving Berlin. The movie was a financial success, earning nearly $10 million for the Army Emergency Relief Fund.

"I Am An American" song sheet. Words and music are by Benjamin Edwards Neal. "I am an American of the U. S. A. My heart thrills with confidence, facing each new day. Saluting the red, white, and blue, I stand loyal to America my native land." Original. 1938.

"ANY BONDS TODAY?" sheet music cover. This theme song of the National Defense Savings Program was composed by Irving Berlin. "ANY BONDS TODAY? Bonds of freedom that's what I'm selling ... ANY BONDS TODAY? Scrape up the most you can–Here comes the freedom man..." Original. 1941.

The year 1942 witnessed the issuance of another "dandy" of a patriotic themed movie, *Yankee Doodle Dandy*. Released by Warner Brothers near Memorial Day, it was a biographical musical based on the life of the iconic song and dance man, George M. Cohan. Actor James Cagney won an Academy Award for his portrayal of Cohan. The movie also garnered three other Oscars, one of which was for Best Music. The song in this film made famous by Cohan was "The Yankee Doodle Boy" derived from the American Revolutionary War song "Yankee Doodle." Other well-known songs from the picture were the patriotic "Over There," "You're A Grand Old Flag," "Mary's A Grand Old Name," "Give My Regards to Broadway," and "Harrigan." In this uplifting patriotic movie, Cagney as Cohan is acting as a song-and-dance version of President Roosevelt and performs the spectacular dance sequence of "The Yankee Doodle Boy."

These two movies brought joy and increased morale for American citizens during the bleakest time of the war, and they have remained prominent in the pantheon of American patriotic films. The only movie to come close was the August 4, 1942, release of Irving Berlin's *Holiday Inn* featuring Bing Crosby and Fred Astaire, which introduced the most memorable holiday song of all, "White Christmas." According to the *Guinness Book of World Records*, the version, as sung by Bing Crosby, has been the world's largest selling single with an estimated 50 million copies sold. The song itself is the single largest seller ever with an estimated 100 million copies sold. While this movie did not have a wartime theme (although a successor 1954 movie, *White Christmas*, did), it featured several of Irving Berlin's songs from prior war-related movies.

These and other movies and songs aided the war effort against the Axis Powers, which finally came to a conclusion in Europe on V-E Day, May 8, 1945, and in Japan on V-J Day, September 2, 1945.

"This is the Army" song sheet for the movie and program from the "All-Soldier Show for the Army Emergency Relief Program." Words and music are by Irving Berlin. "I'm getting tired so I can sleep, I want to sleep so I can dream, I want to dream so that I can be with you." Original. 1942.

"Yankee Doodle Dandy" song sheet from the musical motion picture starring James Cagney and based on the story and music of George M. Cohan. "…but it was Mary, Mary, long before the fashions came; And there is something there that sounds so square, it's a grand old name!" Original. 1942.

Chapter 2

America's Revered Icons

A newly formed and emerging country has to have a symbol, a "mascot," or a suitable icon to project its national image. From May 1607, when the first permanent English settlement was established at Jamestown, Virginia, to July 4, 1776, when Independence was declared from British rule, the American colonies experienced significant growing pains. In the first 170 years as a British colony, the country's inhabitants were subject to many conflicts, especially with the indigenous Indians (Native Americans), in order to protect their domiciles or expand the frontier for additional living space. The most serious armed engagements involved the Wampanoag tribe during King Philip's War in 1675 and the French & Indian War (1754-1763).

The French and Indian War was the name given in the American theater to the conflict between the French and the English and their respective Indian allies for colonial domination. The greater European war was called The Seven-Year War, which pit Great Britain and Prussia against France, Austria, Sweden, and Russia. In North America, due to the explosive expansion of the colonies from about 1700 to 1750, population reached 1.25 million. This created tensions along the boundaries separating New France from the British colonies encompassing most of the Eastern seaboard from Nova Scotia to Virginia. It was along these boundaries that large areas were dominated by various Indian tribes.

During the first four years of this conflict, the British and their Indian allies suffered several defeats at the hand of the French and their Indian allies. During this time, the now newly promoted Colonel George Washington was put in command of the Virginia Regiment, established in 1754 and comprised of prior militia and conscripts. Their mission as part of a larger British force was to march northwest to protect British interests and capture Fort Duquesne at the confluence of the Allegheny and Monongahela Rivers, which form the Ohio River at present-day Pittsburgh. Colonel Washington acted as an aide-de-camp to the British Major-General Braddock, who was the supreme command of all British forces in North America. At the Battle of Monongahela in 1755, General Braddock, using close-order drill tactics in the open, succumbed to the sustained fire from French and Canadian troops using cover. General Braddock and many officers were killed, but Colonel Washington was able to manage a successful retreat that saved many of what was left of the British troops. This disaster was considered to be one of the greatest defeats of Great Britain in the eighteenth century.

After several more British setbacks in 1756 and 1757, William Pitt, a new leader of the British Parliament, came to power and substantially increased military resources to the extent that France was unwilling to match. Due to a British naval blockade, the French were unable to support its troops or add more to replace battle losses. In 1758, the (General) Forbes Expedition pushed the French out of the hotly contested Ohio River Valley with the losses of Fort Duquesne and, in Nova Scotia, the Fortress Louisburg, the latter leading directly to the loss of Quebec City in 1759. In 1760, one of Britain's final victories was the capture of Forts Ticonderoga and Niagara and the eventual capture of Montreal. With Montreal gone, France lost its remaining foothold in Canada and, therefore, North America.

While the fighting was generally over by 1760, the French and Indian War was not formally over until the signing of the Treaty of Paris on February 16, 1763. This war had severe consequences for Great Britain, France, the American colonies, and Native Americans of all loyalties. While Britain gained French Canada and all the areas bounded by the St. Lawrence, Mississippi, and Ohio Rivers, as well as Florida, the war was a financial disaster. Britain's national debt almost doubled, and the country came close to bankruptcy. This forced Great Britain to increase its taxes on the colonies, which ultimately led to the American Revolutionary War in 1775. While France did not consider the loss of its North American territories a big issue, the military losses in the European part of its war and resultant

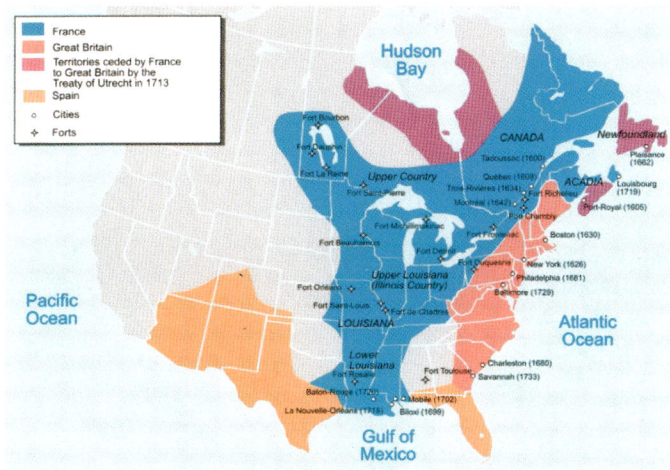

Map showing the distribution of Territorial Holdings by New France, Great Britain, and Spain. Image reproduced from Nouvelle-France map, 1750.

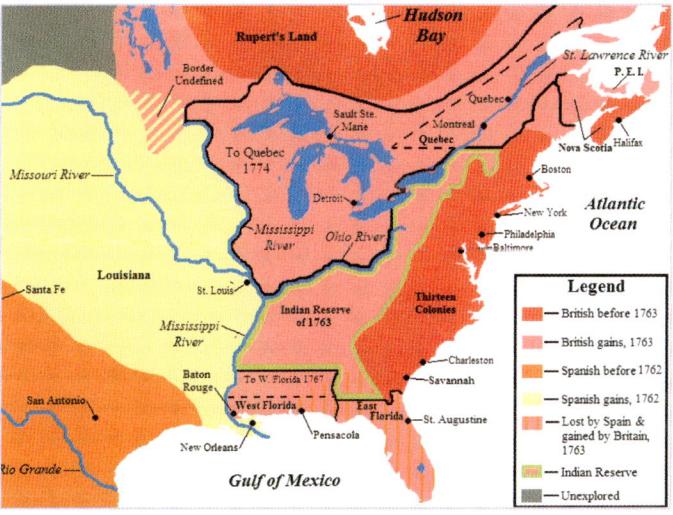

Map showing the distribution of Territorial Gains of Great Britain and Spain following the French and Indian War, 1763. Image based on map drawn by historical artist Jon Platek.

Based on a 1772 portrait of George Washington wearing a colonel's uniform. Painted by Charles Wilson Peale (1741-1827), an American painter, soldier, and naturalist. Washington is portrayed as Colonel of the First Virginia Regiment.

financial burden contributed to the Monarchy being weakened to the point where this led to the French Revolution of 1789. Spain, at little cost, gained the Louisiana territory, but lost Florida to the British.

In 1755, when a youthful George Washington was given a commission as "Colonel of the Virginia Regiment and Commander-in-Chief," he was given the task of defending the western frontiers of Virginia. As the Virginia Regiment was comprised of only full-time American troops, this was the genesis of the American Army. As the Commander of 1,000 regular troops, Washington and his Virginia Regiment participated in more than twenty battles against various Indian tribes as well as taking part in the victorious Forbes Expedition. During this time, Washington was developing a very negative idea of the ad-hoc value of local militias. To Washington the militia recruits were characterized as "loose, idle persons…quite destitute of house and home." These words indicated that Washington considered the local militias to be unreliable, too undisciplined, and too short-term for campaign service requirements. It is interesting that Washington never gained the British Regular Army commission that he requested, and that even his Virginia Regiment officers were considered incompetent by the regular British army officers with whom they served. Certainly both the British and Washington himself had, in the main, contemptuous attitudes towards the value of militia-fighting men; however, of the 42,000 British and colonial militia troops available during the war, about forty percent were local militia — and without them, the British would have had a much worse and longer time subjugating the French.

Due to these thoughts about the perverseness and general incompetence of local militias, the first instance of the term "Yankee Doodle" came into usage. This was the first use of a symbol to represent colonial Americans in general and its fighting men in particular. We know that the verses of the song "Yankee Doodle" were meant to be derisive and mocking towards the colonial troops as unsophisticated country boys (see Chapter One). Therefore, the spread of Yankee Doodle as the first symbol of the spirit of America made little headway except for a caricature image of a cockeyed Yankee Doodle riding a pony.

Brother Jonathan

We all know "Uncle Sam" as the face of America, but it took awhile to get to his persona. The next step in the evolution of the eventual Uncle Sam image was "Brother Jonathan," a fictional character who started out as slogan for the Continental Army during the American Revolutionary War. Between 1776 and 1783, "Brother Jonathan" was one of the less derisive terms used by British-American loyalists to describe their counterparts — the Revolutionary Patriots.

The actual person that may have been the model for Brother Jonathan was a colonial governor by the name of Jonathan Trumbull, Sr. (1710-1785). In 1769, Trumbull became Governor of Connecticut, lasting for fifteen years for both the colony and the state, and stayed in office until 1784. During the American Revolutionary War, Trumbull became a good friend and advisor to General George Washington. Due to the limited resources that the Continental Army had at its disposal, Washington frequently turned to Trumbull for help in mustering more troops or providing provisions for his troops. As the apocryphal story goes, when Washington was faced with a difficult decision in these matters, he was said to say "We must consult Brother Jonathan." As this slogan caught on, it stayed in singular use until the end of the War of 1812. Between the two wars with Great Britain lasting thirty years, Brother Jonathan, as the accepted emblem of a new and vigorous country, was pictured by the illustrators of that era as a political upstart with rustic leanings and devoid of a sense of personal dignity.

After the War of 1812, the image of Brother Jonathan as a less-dignified person began to share some space with a new upstart symbol — the more dignified Uncle Sam and, to some extent, the feminine symbol Columbia. However, Brother Jonathan was not quite through. Even though the Uncle Sam characterization was making great progress through the illustrated newspapers of the American Civil War era, Brother Jonathan was still enjoying "print" well into the end of the nineteenth century.

For the 125 years that illustrators have portrayed Brother Jonathan in a myriad of situations, he has, for the most part, either been pictured as clean-shaven or with some sort of the goatee, given a relatively youthful persona with a beguiling smile, and sometimes smoking a thin cigar. His wearing apparel has also undergone change. Alternatively he has been shown to wear either a long brim, flat, crown hat or, more often, a top hat. His coat has been typically a buttoned jacket with long tails over a star-decorated shirt with a vest and long-striped red and white pants, some with stirrups. These characteristics are what we would commonly associate with Uncle Sam.

"The War in Europe." This engraved illustration depicts John Bull (Great Britain) being restrained by Brother Jonathan, sitting on the rock of "non-intervention," during the fighting for the unification of Italy, which became a nation-state March 17, 1861. *Harper's Weekly*.

Punch, May 23, 1896. *Punch* was an English satire magazine that usually used Brother Jonathan as the symbol of America. Titled "Jonathan's Latest," the illustration depicts a hostile and armed Brother Jonathan trying to grab "Cuba" away from "Spain" with the background image of Christopher Columbus intoning "Had I foreseen it would have come to this…I would have never discovered America!" The Spanish-American War began two years later on April 25, 1898. 8.5" x 11"

Uncle Sam

Puck, June 1876. This engraved illustration shows Brother Jonathan welcoming the personifications of many of the invited countries to the Centennial International Exhibition of 1876, which celebrated the 100th Anniversary of the United States as a Republic. Eleven countries had their own exhibition buildings including Great Britain, Japan, and Brazil. 12" x 7.5"

Harper's Weekly, October 6, 1877. This engraved illustration, "Our Flag is Still There," depicts Brother Jonathan holding a rifle in one hand while holding a sign with the other hand that reads: "In the name of the United States of America to the Riflemen of the World." The background imagery shows "the rockets' red glare, the bombs bursting in air" over Fort McHenry in September 1814, during the Battle of 1812 fought against the British. 10.5" x 15.5"

The story of Uncle Sam's genesis is well known, but it bears repeating: During the War of 1812, the Northern and Western parts of the state of New York were within the theater of war due to British naval squadrons located in and around the St. Lawrence Seaway. Lake Champlain, in the northern part of the state, was a hotly contested area between American and British naval forces. Troy, New York, was located directly south of this northern engagement zone and its location on the Hudson River made it a well-situated Quartermaster supply point. Samuel Wilson, a local meat packer and inspector of meat products, was assigned to inspect all meat purchased for the Government during the War of 1812. Once Wilson certified that the meat was of the quality specified, he stamped "U. S." on each barrel.

Samuel Wilson (September 13, 1766 - July 31, 1854) was commonly called "Uncle Sam" by his friends. When a workman inquired as to what the initials "U. S." meant, another workman jocularly replied, "I don't know, unless they mean Uncle Sam." Before long the initials of the United States were regarded as "Uncle Sam," and this popular nomenclature has been in use ever since. Interestingly, the U. S. Naval forces, outmanned three to one, scored a decisive victory over the British at the Battle of Plattsburgh (Lake Champlain) on September 14, 1814, thus putting an end to the War of 1812.

Soon after Samuel Wilson's Quartermaster business came to an end, but his "Uncle Sam" legacy has survived. Troy, New York, lays claim to being the historic home of Uncle Sam. Due to Samuel Wilson's unintentional contribution, his birthday is celebrated every year on September 13th. On September 15, 1961, the 87th United States Congress adopted a resolution: "Resolved by the Senate and the House of Representatives that the Congress salutes Uncle Sam Wilson of Troy, New York as the progenitor of America's National symbol of Uncle Sam." The city of Troy also houses the Uncle Sam Foundation of Troy, New York, which has virtually everything anyone would want to know about the life and times of Uncle Sam Wilson and his alter ego.

"Greetings from Troy, N.Y., Home of Uncle Sam." This is where the familiar sobriquet "Uncle Sam" was first used in 1812. Published by Joe Connors, Averill Park, New York.

A fierce-looking Uncle Sam holds aloft a billowing American Flag while exhorting the citizens to "Buy War Bonds!" c. early 1940s poster. 13" x 19"

Uncle Sam's Image

Through a succession of illustrators stemming from the early American Civil War years, the first images of Uncle Sam took a similar track as Brother Jonathan. The main illustrator "to capture" Uncle Sam and preserve his identity for the ages was Thomas Nast. In 1861, the first documented illustration of Uncle Sam was published in the pages of *Harper's Weekly*. Several more followed over the years; drawn by mainly unknown illustrators each adding a layer to flesh out an evolving icon. It was the Thanksgiving issue of *Harper's Weekly*, dated November 30, 1869, that Nast first drew an Uncle Sam image, but not one that we would be familiar with today. Aside from Uncle Sam's prosaic image, the overall illustration was not just another throw-down Thanksgiving illustration. Nast portrayed the scene in such a way that it spoke volumes about the emerging characterization that personified Uncle Sam's presence as America's spokesman. However, "Uncle Sam" was more than just a spokesman: "he" was on his way to becoming a unifying symbol of freedom and equality.

According to experts that study semiotics, or the science of symbols, both Brother Jonathan and Uncle Sam are considered to be a form of symbol called metonymy, which is a connotation of one thing being substituted for another, i.e. Uncle Sam for the United States. In comparing Uncle Sam to Brother Jonathan, there emerged decided differences in dress and behavior. After coexisting together for decades, the mature, dignified version of Uncle Sam, as drawn in the later years by Nast and others, became the definitive image. By the mid-1870s these images featured Uncle Sam with red and white striped pants with stirrups, a blue waistcoat with long tails, a white star decorated blue vest, white shirt with a red or black floppy bow tie, and a large stovepipe top hat blue or white in color with a decorative hat band. He was a literal "walking-talking" American flag. In retrospect, Brother Jonathan was depicted as a clean-shaven, somewhat unkempt rustic symbol of the "people" whereas the maturing image of Uncle Sam was a lanky, bewhiskered, stern image of "getting the job done." Uncle Sam was the national personification of the best ideals of our "country" — the United States of America.

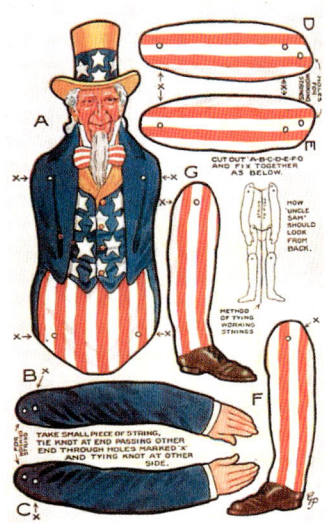

Postcard of an Uncle Sam Paper Doll Cut-Out. Instructions for the construction of the paper doll are written on the card. Published by W. E. Mack, London; "Toy Town" Series No. 064. This extremely rare cutout postcard is valued over $1,000.

Cartoon image of Uncle Sam. Samuel Wilson, a native of Arlington, Mass., was called Uncle Sam by his friends. Sam Wilson became an inspector of supplies for the government during the War of 1812 and stamped all that he inspected "U. S." for United States. Soldiers began referring to items so marked as belonging to "Uncle Sam." The image of Uncle Sam has changed over time. In the beginning, he was unshaven and wearing a tail coat and top hat; red pants were added during Andrew Jackson's Presidency. During the Civil War, a beard was added... Thus a symbol of the United States was born. Art by Bam Sawler. Published by Yankee Colour Corp.

Uncle Sam with his serving tray: "I thought I was serving Uncle Sam: T'ain't so: He's serving me the best of the land." Artist signed Bernhardt Wall. Publisher unknown. 1919.

Huld's Postcard Puzzle Series No. 30; completed image is 5" x 14" and each card has an appropriate quote. TOP CARD: "The first card shows Uncle Sam smiling bright, because he knows he is Allright (sic)." SECOND CARD: "Here are more of the stars, also the shield, In the battle for honor he never will yield." THIRD CARD: "The stripes forever, long may they wave, 'O'er the land of the free and the home of the brave." BOTTOM CARD: He stands firm on his feet since his birth; They are large enough to cover the earth." This set was published by Franz Huld and is extremely rare.

Campaign postcard. Uncle Sam wearing both William Jennings Bryan and William Howard Taft buttons in the November 1908 Presidential election: "Which? Gosh, I'm for BILL.." Published by Franz Huld Co., 1908.

Real Photo Postcards (RPPC) of William Smith (1819-1908), native of the Catskill Mountain area, New York State, as an accurate representation of "Uncle Sam." Publisher unknown.

Harper's Weekly, November 20, 1869. Engraved illustration of "Uncle Sam's Thanksgiving Dinner": This was the very first depiction of Uncle Sam by Thomas Nast. His illustration espoused universal suffrage among all people of the world. "Come One Come All" and "Free and Equal." 15.5" x 10.5"

Frank Leslie's Illustrated Newspaper, November 26, 1887: Engraved illustration of "Thanksgiving Day 1887" shows an allegorical symbol of Uncle Sam riding on an overflowing cornucopia drawn by tethered turkeys. A handcuffed figure, depicting Anarchy, can be seen on the ground. 10.5" x 15.5"

Uncle Sam & the End of the 19th Century

The decades from 1890 through 1920 could be called the Emergence of Modern America. The years from 1890 into the very early 1900s were among the most interesting in the history of the United States due to the problems arising from rapid industrialization, urbanization (1890 Census: 63 million), increasing immigration (15 million in 1920), and pervasive corruption in the worlds of business and politics. At this time America's literacy rate was only 13.5%. Also, it was estimated that, similar to today, 99% of the nation's wealth was held by 1% of the population including names like Andrew Carnegie, J. P. Morgan, John Rockefeller, and Cornelius Vanderbilt.

In the book *American Colossus: The Triumph of Capitalism, 1865-1900*, the author opines that there were two problems with the ascendency of capitalism in what he called the Decade of the Century: (1) How to maintain the "national identity" in the face of rapid expansion of immigration and a derisive political environment that catered to widespread corruption among the powerful elite; and (2) How to manage the increasingly powerful and profitable economic base made possible by the benefits of the Industrial Revolution without succumbing to the corrosive effects of a powerful Progressive social activist base that was in many cases radicalizing and co-opting the labor movement. Some of the main economic factors that changed the complexity of the 1890s were the passage of the Sherman Anti-Trust Act of 1890 (limit the power of corporations that controlled a high percentage of market share), the Panic of 1893 (four years of depression), Coxey's Army (of the unemployed) protest march on Washington D. C. of 1894, and three deleterious strikes: Carnegie Steel Company of 1892, the Pullman Railcar Company of 1894, and the Bituminous and Anthracite Coal strikes of 1898, 1900, and 1902.

Puck, May 29, 1895. Chromolithographic illustration "Progress and Poverty – A Decoration Day Study": Depicts a forlorn Uncle Sam holding the sign "I Am Busted" and holding his hat labeled "Deficit." In front of him, the well-off Army of Pensioners are marching with the banner "We will continue to save the country, so long as there is a Dollar in the Treasury" in order to pay their pensions. The Panic of 1893, caused in part by the lack of silver coinage in circulation in favor of a gold standard, enabled a new financial panic that seized the international markets and caused a massive loss of confidence in the dollar. Thus the U. S. Treasury had barely enough gold reserve to redeem dollars for gold. Artist: Dalrymple. Centerfold, 20" x 13"

Puck, early 1900s. Chromolithographic illustration "The Fool Pied Piper": An American patriotically dressed pied-piper drawing all of the cut-throats and anarchists from Europe and promising emigration into the United States with the beckoning Statue of Liberty in the background. The cheering representatives of the different countries are happy to be rid of these rats that allegedly belonged to terrorist organizations such as the infamous "Black Hand," a Serbian group responsible for assassinating the Archduke Franz Ferdinand of Austria in Sarajevo, Bosnia, and Herzegovina, which instigated World War I. Centerfold, 20" x 13"

Judge, 1891. Chromolithographic illustration "Coming Before The People Again": Depicts Uncle Sam in an easy-chair smirking at the symbol of the Democratic Administration under Grover Cleveland (1885-1889) with little accomplishments versus the accomplishments achieved by the Republican Administration (1890) in one year under President Benjamin Harrison (1889-1893). Artist: Hamilton. Centerfold, 20" x 13"

Harper's Weekly, July 1895. Engraved illustration "The Glorious Fourth": Uncle Sam and Columbia cheer on the marching "Industrial Army--July 4, 1895" ... workers and businessmen who all wish a revival of business to strengthen the dollar in order to pay wages. The resultant business depression from the Panic of 1893 exacerbated working conditions, which led to some serious strikes. This is compared to the upper drawing that depicts the woebegone Coxey's Army of the unemployed with their failed March on Washington D.C. in 1894. Artist: W. A. Rogers. 11" x 15"

When President William McKinley took office in March 1897, America's Age of Imperialism began. In 1896, under President Grover Cleveland, there was a debate about what action the United States should take with respect to Cuba, a large Spanish territorial Island just a short distance from Florida. Since America was becoming an emerging industrial power, the need for raw materials and commodities became urgent. Therefore, it was thought by the expansionists that Cuba would fit the country's needs and, in February 1896, Congress passed a resolution affirming the United States' support to the Cuban rebels and offering aid to Spain in negotiating a peace settlement for Cuba (the offer was rejected).

After McKinley became President, the Republican Congress passed a resolution in which the United States formally recognized the independence of the Republic of Cuba. After negotiations with Spain broke down with the explosion and loss of the *USS Maine* battleship, an ultimatum was issued to Spain coincident with a naval blockade. With Spain's refusal to vacate Cuba, Congress declared war. The resultant short war with Spain began on April 25, 1898, and ended on August 12, 1898, with the United States victorious. McKinley's Secretary of State, John Hay, called it a "splendid little war." While Cuba was being secured, the Navy's Asiatic Squadron, under Admiral Dewey, made short work of the Spanish Fleet off the Philippine Islands. At the conclusion of the Spanish-American War, through the Treaty of Paris (December 10, 1898), the United States annexed the Philippines and gained possession of Guam and Puerto Rico (for a payment of $20 million to Spain) as well as political and economic control over Cuba. Unfortunately, the United States got itself embroiled in a conflict with the Philippine Nationalists, which caused a second war — the Philippine-American War — that ended on July 4, 1902 with additional scattered fighting with the Moros until 1913.

LIFE, April 13, 1899. Illustration "Glimpses Into the Future—1976: The Last American": The "last American" is surrounded by a derisive crowd of immigrants with the background of an Arabic-looking building. In the period 1894-1899 immigration into the United States averaged 276,500 annually with 32% from Central and Eastern Europe, 22% from Southern Europe, and 12% from Ireland. After 1900, nativists concerns about rampant immigration did not do much to stem immigration.
Artist: F. W. Read. 8.5" x 11"

Judge, March 21, 1891. Chromolithographic illustration "Awakening the Giant": A bruised and battered Uncle Sam, in the uniform of a U. S. Marine, rests on a rock dated "1861." This date represents the fact that at the start of the American Civil War, the U. S. Navy only had forty-two commission vessels, of which thirty-nine were available for home waters duty. Of these there were only four Ships-of-the-Line carrying eighty-four guns with an average age of forty-five years. Added to that problem were the many U. S. Naval Officers resigning their commissions to return to the Confederacy. Thirty years later the U. S. Navy was still not up to the task and Columbia states: "Awake and resume your proper position as one of the greatest of Maritime Powers!" President Benjamin Harrison (1889-1893) was shown backing Columbia's "wake-up" call up with subsidies to rapidly construct modern warships and the acquisition of bases to maintain the U. S. Fleet in foreign seas. Artist: Victor. 10" x 13.5"

Puck, November 13, 1895. Chromolithographic illustration "Uncle Sam's Dream of Conquest and Carnage–Caused by Reading the Jingo Newspapers." A dreaming Uncle Sam with his thoughts (from the top clockwise): "Sweeping his enemies from the seas;" "Kicking John Bull out of his boots"; "Establishing formidable and invulnerable coast defenses"; "Showing the whole world that he knows his rights and will maintain them at all hazards"; and "Annexing all outlying countries." This illustration was drawn before the United States actually embarked on some of the mentioned measures. Artist: Keppler. Centerfold, 20.5" x 14"

Puck, April 6, 1901. Chromolithographic illustration "Columbia's Easter Bonnet": Columbia, dressed in a patriotic naval uniform, tries on her bonnet topped with a four-gunned ship "World Power" belching "expansion" smoke. Harrison's subsidies proved very beneficial as the U. S. Navy now had a complement of six battleships and two armored cruisers. Several of these ships rendered valuable service in the Spanish-American War.
Artist: Dalrymple. 10" x 13.5"

Puck, May 29, 1895. This chromolithographic illustration, "The Wars That Never Come," shows Senators Hoar and Henry Cabot Lodge of Massachusetts and Financier J.P. Morgan lamenting the fact that "we've been watching matters sadly and noted, too, with tears, that of wars we've wanted badly there isn't one appears…" Conflicts did not occur in the Republic of Hawaii, the Bering Sea over fishing rights, and Nicaragua, where a possible canal was to be dug. Overlooking the three Jingos is the image of Peace holding an olive branch. *Puck*, with a liberal, Democratic purview, was anti-imperialistic. Artist: Keppler. 10.5" x 14".

Puck, January 1, 1896. Chromolithographic illustration "The Nation's Holiday Feast": Uncle Sam gives a toast… "I'm at peace with my neighbors–and they're a horde, But our peace isn't peace at the point of the sword; I don't want their land or their wares, I mind my business, and they mind theirs… Here's to drink: 'Peace to All!'" The table's well-armed guests are France, England, Turkey, Russia, Germany, Italy, and the mischievous Puck. Artist: C. Y. Taylor. Centerfold, 21" x 14"

Puck, February 26, 1896. Chromolithographic illustration "After the Carnival": Uncle Sam after a night of carousing and saber rattling… "By Jingo, it was a great racket!–but I showed 'em the kind of stuff I'm made of, anyhow!–I wonder how John (Bull) feels?" Artist: Fred Opper. 10" x 12"

Puck, November 24, 1897. Chromolithographic illustration "Spain's New Street Crier–With the same old cry!": Uncle Sam glaringly looking on at the "Peace Pronouncements" of the two Spanish negotiators, Praxedes Mateo Sagasta and Ramon Blanco y Erenas, while European leaders look on approvingly. Up to this point American and Spanish negotiators were trying to hammer out a peaceful solution to the Spanish hold on Cuba. Sagasta, now Spain's Prime Minister, was willing to agree to Cuban autonomy as of January 1, 1898. However, early in 1898, a riot broke out in Havana that caused the United States to move the *USS Maine* to the Havana Harbor to protect U. S. citizens when the *Maine* suffered a deadly explosion – and that was the causal effect that started the Spanish-American War in April 1898. Artist: J. S. Pughe. Centerfold, 21" x 14"

Boston Globe, May 28, 1898. Engraved illustration "Well, I Hardly Know Which To Take First!": Uncle Sam deciding what to select on the Bill of Fare with President McKinley ready to take his order as a waiter. At this point in McKinley's administration, the United States was involved in a short war with Spain and in forty days the Republic of Hawaii would be annexed. Apparently Uncle Sam selected the whole menu. 10" x 8"

"Don't be afraid Uncle – We'll get there all right." Teddy Roosevelt and Uncle Sam sitting in a patriotic embellished car with a dog and a chicken getting out of the way of the speed demons. Embossed with gold highlights. Published by Fred Lounsbury. Lounsbury (1857-1917) worked in the paper novelty business which included souvenir postcards. Most of Lounsbury's postcard sets have four cards each. This postcard belonged to an unnumbered set of four all with the image of Uncle Sam.

Patriotic Covers–Set of Four: All have humorous Uncle Sam caricatures showing the symbols of Spain being harassed.

Judge, June 4, 1898. Chromolithography illustration: A large-scale caricature of a winking Uncle Sam saying "Well, friend John, 'THERE ARE OTHERS,'" in response to John Bull's declaration that "The Sun Never Sets on British Possessions." In the background is the American flag on the Philippines. At this time the Spanish-American War was not yet over, so the flag flying over the Philippines was presumptuous. Artist: Victor Gillam. 10" x 13"

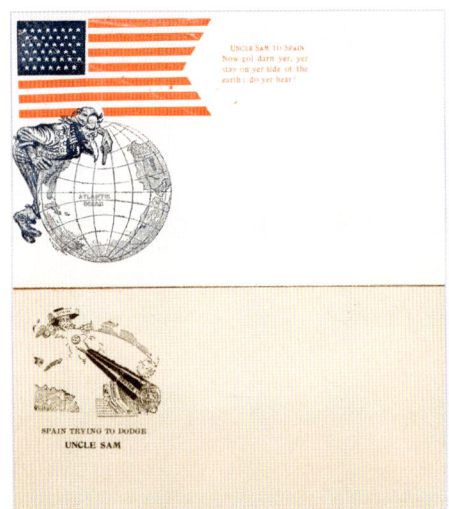

Patriotic Covers: (1) "On To Havana!" Uncle Sam… "See here Alphonsee you've played around here long enough, you'll have to come out." (2) "On To Porto Rico." Uncle Sam to Spain… "I've a nice little new cradle for you."

Patriotic Covers: (1) "A Bitter Pill Senor, But You Must Swallow It." Uncle Sam's Prescription--a Peace Terms pill; (2) Uncle Sam is shooting his gun through the Spanish flag while the Spaniard's gun misfires.

Patriotic Covers: (1) With the backdrop of a 46-star American flag, Uncle Sam is leaning over the sphere telling Spain… "Now gol darn yer, yer stay on yer side of the earth; do yer here?" (2) "Spain Trying to Dodge Uncle Sam's Artillery Shells."

Uncle Sam writes at his desk "By the Grace of God, Free and Independent" as he watches the boys outside playing with fireworks instead of having to go to war and fire an actual cannon. Postcard is embossed with gold highlights. Published by Fred Lounsbury, 1907.

Puck, 1900. Chromolithographic illustration, "Declined With Thanks," showing Uncle Sam as a very portly gentleman being measured by President McKinley for a new set of clothes so that Uncle Sam can expand even more. Bolts of cloth are titled "Enlightened," "Foreign Policy," and "Rational Expansion." The Anti-expansionists say: "Here, take a dose of this anti-fat and get thin again." Uncle Sam replies… "No, Sonny! I never did take any of that stuff, and I'm too old to begin!" Artist: J. S. Pughe. Centerfold, 21" x 14"

"Now, once again–altogether Boys! Siss! Boom!! A-h!!!" Uncle Sam is seated while children representing Cuba, Hawaii, Puerto Rico, Philippines, and Guam celebrate with firecrackers around him. Postcard is embossed with gold highlights. Published by Fred Lounsbury, 1907.

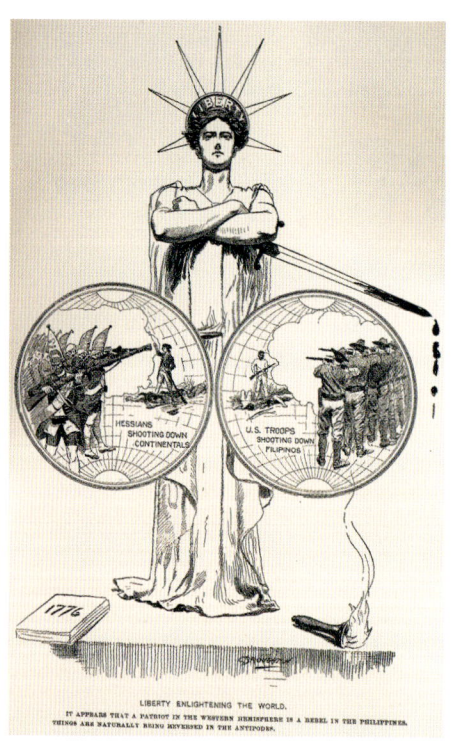

LIFE, April 13, 1899. Drawn illustration "The Imperial Robes": Uncle Sam, dressed as an Imperial Roman Senator, asks… "Say, LIFE, How Do I Look?" LIFE responds… "You Look Like A D--- Fool." Uncle Sam also has a lease and a ball and chain tied to a native. This was the mid-point of President McKinley's administration and the United States had already annexed or purchased Cuba, Puerto Rico, Guam, and Hawaii. Artist: F. T. Richarof. 8.5" x 11"

LIFE, April 13, 1899. Drawn illustration, "Liberty Enlightening the World," showing twin cameos of the "Hessians Shooting Down Continentals" and "U. S. Troops Shooting Down Filipinos." Liberty says: "It appears that a patriot in the western hemisphere is a rebel in the Philippines, things are naturally being reversed in the Antipodes." Artist: Broughton.

Engraved illustration "WHITHER?" That is the question confronting the caricature of a stern looking Uncle Sam at the crossroads leading to a passive foreign policy in upholding the Monroe Doctrine or following an aggressive foreign policy by annexing and purchasing foreign territories. 8" x 12". Artist: Berrymon, 1898.

ADDING TO THE GAYETY OF THE NATIONS.

A DANGEROUS PERFORMANCE BY AN AMATEUR.

While the United States was in the throes of annexing the recent territorial gains derived from the Spanish-American War in late 1898, the expansionist policies of a regenerated United States was not over. Since the early 1880s, the Hawaiian Island chain, located in the mid-Pacific Ocean, was being coveted by European countries such as Great Britain, France, and Russia. In order to forestall annexations of the Islands by foreign powers, in 1849 the U. S. concluded a treaty of friendship that served as the initiation of official relations with the Hawaiian Monarchy. The next forty years proved to be an economic boom for Hawaii; it became a major coaling station for American whalers as well as expanding its sugar cane production for world markets. In the early 1890s, with American interests dominating Island politics, the reigning Monarch, Queen Liliuokalani, tried to offset this trend by strengthening the weakening monarchy. This failed when the American planters' interests, led by Samuel Dole (Pineapple), deposed the Queen in 1893 and established a local pro-American annexation government. When the current U. S. President, Grover Cleveland, opposed this coup, Dole declared Hawaii an independent republic. The next U. S. President, William McKinley, spurred on by nationalist fervor over the recent victories in the Spanish-American War, gave his approval to annex Hawaii in 1898. In 1900, Hawaii was made a territory of the United States and, on November 11, 1909, the U. S. established a naval base at Pearl Harbor.

Throughout the 1890s many cartoonists of the leading newspapers and satire magazines took to task the United States' designs on foreign territories and aggressive expansion tendencies. *Puck* magazine was probably one of the most daring in portraying caricatures of political figures in comic situations due to the liberal orientation of the magazine. Illustrative satire was a popular medium for the expression of intellectual politics. To this extent Uncle Sam, and Columbia to some small degree, were the sources of much humor. Also since mass production of postcards was not yet viable, in order for people to express their patriotism concerning the Spanish-American War, they, instead, sent mail with cacheted patriotic slogans and sayings.

LIFE, April 13, 1899. Drawn illustration, "Adding to the Gayety of the Nations: A Dangerous Performance by an Amateur," depicts Uncle Sam as a Pierrot-type comical caricature juggling battleships, Cuba, soldiers, trusts, Porto Rico, and the Philippines while balancing on the earth's sphere attached to a tightrope named "Humanity."

Reproduction photograph: Hawaii State Library, Honolulu, Hawaii, circa 1910.

Puck, March 25, 1903. Chromolithographic illustration "His Neighborly Suggestion": A stern Uncle Sam, leaning on a shovel, admonishes a diminutive Central America revolutionary… "Now, young man, while I'm digging here, I'd like a long period of depression in the Revolution Business." Treaties were signed in November 1903 to begin construction of the Panama Canal. Artist: J. S. Pughe. 10.5" x 13.5"

Given the monetary benefits attributable to world trade between the Atlantic and Pacific oceans, there was always interest in building a canal linking the two oceans across the Isthmus of Panama. After many studies, the French, under Ferdinand de Lesseps, started construction of a sea level canal on January 1, 1880. Nine years later the French abandoned the project due to poor construction techniques and its workforce being decimated by the diseases of malaria and yellow fever that contributed to 22,000 deaths. After much diplomatic wrangling, which included the recognition of the new country of Panama due to its split from Columbia on November 3, 1903, the United States, under the new administration of President Theodore Roosevelt, signed treaties to initiate the construction of a new canal with locks on November 6, 1903. The United States also provided troops to quell any unrest from Columbia to take over the canal site. (In 1921, the United States paid Columbia $10 million for its recognition of Panama). The United States purchased the construction equipment from the French for $40 million and began work on May 4, 1904. After a little more of ten years of construction, the 47.9-mile Panama Canal was completed with the first transit occurring on August 15, 1914.

LIFE, 1903. Drawn illustration "Alas, Poor de Lesseps!": Uncle Sam ruminates over the allegorical skull of Ferdinand de Lesseps, the French engineer who initially started construction on the Panama Canal only to fail with 22,000 deaths to show for it. Artist: Broughton. 10.5" x 14.5"

After Theodore (Teddy) Roosevelt assumed the Presidency on September 14, 1901 due to the assassination of President McKinley, his two terms in office were marked with a rather aggressive policy called the Big Stick Diplomacy. This slogan was used as a corollary to the existing Monroe Doctrine, a policy established in 1823 that any intervention by foreign powers in the politics of the Americas is potentially a hostile act against the United States. The Big Stick, therefore, referred to the proverb: "Speak softly and carry a big stick; you will go far." This diplomacy was used in the Venezuelan Affair (1902), the building of the Panama Canal (1903), and the holding a form of hegemony over the Cuban affairs (1901).

Another form of diplomacy first instigated from President Roosevelt that prospered under President William Taft was the Dollar Diplomacy, which was a means of maintaining political stability in Central America and certain places in East Asia, especially China, by guaranteeing loans made to them by foreign bankers and, thereby, keep economic leverage in their affairs. China was the "apple in the eye" of many foreign powers, including the United States, as an opening to that market portended possible economic gains, but that possibility ended with the rise of a proto-nationalistic group called the "Boxers." The Boxer Rebellion started in 1899 and ended in 1901 with a victory by the Eight-Nation Alliance. The Rebellion's leaders were against foreign imperialism, Christian evangelism and missionaries, and opium. One term that was used by the Chinese Mandarin officials was "carving the melon" — an inference that the newly converted Chinese Christians were behind the imperialists attempts to divide and colonize China piece by piece. Finally the Foreign Legation in Beijing was relieved by 20,000 Alliance troops and the rebellion came to an end. China was now in a more weakened position and thus open to further "spheres of influence" called the Open Door Policy; this policy indicated that the United States and other European Powers could trade with China on an equal basis while affirming that China's independence and integrity would be honored. After World War I was concluded, the Open Door Policy was reaffirmed at the Washington (D.C.) Conference (1921-1922).

Puck, 1904. Chromolithographic illustration "The Big Stick in the Caribbean Sea": President Theodore Roosevelt carries a "big stick" while aggressively marching in the Caribbean Sea towing his fleet of armored cruisers. Artist: W. A. Rogers.

Puck, February 2, 1898. Chronographic illustration "Commerce vs. Conquest": Uncle Sam and John Bull, dressed in naval uniforms, approach a frightened Chinese Mandarin who was initially scared by the bellicose attitudes of armed Germany, France, and Russia. Uncle Sam whispers to John Bull… "Don't scare him, John, the way those other fellows are doing. Tell him all we want is to have him open his harbors and markets to everybody!" Artist: Dalrymple. Centerfold, 21" x 14"

Puck, 1899. Lithographic illustration "Putting His Foot Down": A stern and militarily dressed Uncle Sam holds a "Trade Treaty with China" while standing on a map of China. He lectures the assembled powers (Germany, Italy, England, Austria, Russia, and France), each of which have large shears, by saying… "Gentlemen, you may cut up the map as much as you like; but remember that I'm here to stay, and that you can't divide me up into spheres of influence!" The Boxer Rebellion started in 1899 and did not end until 1901. Artist: J. S. Pughe.

In the very early years of the twentieth century, when the United States was positioning itself as an emerging world leader, other European colonial powers such as Great Britain, France, Germany, and Russia were having their share of problems with one another or with their respective colonies in terms of trade and empire dominance. Great Britain was especially having difficulties stemming from their sanguine "victory" in the Anglo-Boer War (1899-1902) in South Africa. Prior to this episode, Great Britain, like the United States, was experiencing a foreign policy based on a state of "splendid isolation." This meant that as the greatest colonial power in the world, Britain did not see the need to rely on other countries, but that also meant that they did not have any allies. The Anglo-Boer War changed that mind-set with the knowledge that if any one of the Continental powers, especially Germany (who had colonies in Africa), intervened on the part of the Boers, Britain would have been in a "splendid mess." Due to the conduct of the British during the war, especially with regards to their "scorched earth" policies, there was a wave of Anglophobia across the Continent. The general feeling was that Britain was doing "a bit of bullying" and had to be put in her place, at least euphemistically.

In Britain, there were a series of postcards issued that reflected the fact that the United States, France, Germany, and Russia were using their collective might to "isolate" Great Britain from many trade alliances. Arthur Moreland, an English illustrator of political cartoons and caricatures, drew many political propaganda postcards featuring John Bull (personification of Britain) being bullied on the economy and trade by Uncle Sam (America), Germany, France, and Russia. Moreland, in many ways, was the Thomas Nast of his era.

The Entente Cordiale, signed April 4, 1904, was a series of agreements between Great Britain and France that brought both powers out of their isolationistic shells, reinstated their historic friendship after one hundred years of intermittent conflict, and resolved their problems with regard to colonial matters. This agreement paved the way for these two countries to become part of the Triple Alliance against Germany in World War I.

Artist: Arthur Moreland. Published by C. W. Faulkner & Co., London; Series No. 248.

John Bull (English) asking: "If you please gentlemen, may I sit down somewhere?" The Chorus of Foreigners (U.S., Germany, and France) responds, "Yes, try the corner."

John Bull, as a General Merchant, is crowded out by Russian, U.S., French, and German products. "Here, I say, this is a free country I know, but I'm not going to have your stalls right in front of my shop."

An effort was made by Great Britain to replace traditional free trade with a policy of protective duties. The foreigners (Russia, France, Germany, and United States) respond, "Now then John, move up."

John Bull (English): "It's my own island you know Gentlemen." Response from the Foreigners (USA, Russia, Germany, Spain, and France): "Can't help it John, we must live, and you invited us." Britain, at the time (early 1900s), as a world colonial power was somewhat removed from the other leading countries, so the leaders of the four largest European countries and the USA were using their collective might to isolate Britain from world trade.

John Bull (English): "I say this is getting serious." John Bull is standing in the middle of piled boxes sent to him from his foreign competition. The sign behind him says: "John Bull's International Dumping Ground." The boxes represent excess or surplus materials dumped on him by his foreign protagonists changing the balance of trade.

Uncle Sam & the 20th Century

When World War I began, America pledged neutrality. The United States did send aid to Great Britain in spite of Germany's warning that all transatlantic shipping, neutral or not, was subject to attack. On May 7, 1915, the *RMS Lusitania* was sunk by one or more torpedoes from a German submarine off the southern coast of Ireland with a loss of life of nearly 1,500 passengers and crew including 128 Americans. This was probably the single most important event that brought the United States into the war on the side of the Triple Entente allies. By now Woodrow Wilson was President, elected on his neutrality platform of keeping the United States out of foreign wars. However, after the sinking of the Lusitania, the United States knew it was going to be impossible to avoid war, so the country was put on a war footing and a draft was instigated. In the next two years postcards and images of Uncle Sam that were once nuanced became more focused and serious against the enlarging threat of Germany.

"Our Boys on the Job." A World War I "doughboy" carrying the flag of "Liberty" confronts a battered-looking German. Artist: Stockwell. Published by Palmer Publishing Co., New York.

"When THIS GENTLEMAN takes off his coat – he means business." Uncle Sam showing his muscle as the United States exerts its power in World War I. Published by Illustrated Postal Card & Novelty Co.

"That's my Uncle Sam and maybe I'm not proud of him." This thought represented a large but passive anti-war sentiment in the United States before World War I. Published by Illustrated Postal Card & Novelty Co.

The lighthouse beacon shines on the American flag as the ship patrols our shores. Uncle Sam is observing the ship with his telescope… "Oh! Say can you see." Artist signed Gesner. Publisher is unknown.

"L'Oncle Sam" (Uncle Sam). Uncle Sam says in response to Kaiser Wilhelm, "A Guillaume qui sollicite son intervention." (To William who is asking for intervention), Mon cher, le temps, c'est de l'argent, je n'en ai pas a perdre! (My friend, time is money and I do not have any to lose!) Artist: A. P. Larry. Series Humoristique de la Guerre, 1914.

"Ils Trop Verts!" (They are too green!). Uncle Sam is pointing out to Kaiser Wilhelm that the hanging grapes from the cups titled Warsaw, London, Calais, Dunkirk, and Paris are too green to pick, meaning that Wilhelm is too optimistic about conquering those cities before a certain date. Published by Revanche #177; Rare hand-tinted card.

The Independent (which incorporated *Harper's Weekly*), March 16, 1918. "WHO SAID PEACE?: A mad Uncle Sam rolling up his sleeve while brandishing a cutlass. Artist: W. C. Morris. 8.5" x 11.5"

The Independent, June 30, 1917. A stern Uncle Sam, holding a sword in one hand while waving to Britannia of England, is saying: "Hold The Fort! I Am Coming!" On April 6, 1917, the United States declared war on Germany. Artist: W. C. Morris. 8.5" x 11.5"

"I Want YOU for the U. S. Army"

It goes without saying that the most famous poster in the world is the… "I Want YOU for the U. S. Army." Painted by its creator, James Montgomery Flagg, in 1916, the colorful drawing was originally published for the July 6, 1916, issue of *Leslie's Weekly*. The title for the magazine was "What Are You Doing for Preparedness?" The portrait of Uncle Sam, in this stern image, sold more than four million copies that were printed between 1917 and 1918 as the United States was entering World War I. This image of Uncle Sam was the most important in the pantheon of portrayals that personified the United States. Flagg's poster, drawn to encourage recruitment in the United States Army during World War I, showed Uncle Sam pointing at the viewer with the famous and immortal caption: "I Want YOU for the U. S. Army." James Montgomery Flagg (1877-1960), an important American artist and illustrator, used his own face for his portrait of Uncle Sam, adding "age" and a white goatee as he was only thirty-nine years old at that time. All-in-all Flagg contributed forty-six works to support the Great War effort. *Leslie's Weekly* continued to use the visage of Uncle Sam in many circumstances on its covers during 1917 and 1918.

"I WANT YOU FOR U. S. ARMY nearest recruiting station." This poster represents the most successful painting of the iconic Uncle Sam image ever drawn. Reproduction. Artist: James Montgomery Flagg. 1916. 24" x 30"

Leslie's, July 6, 1916. "What Are YOU Doing For Preparedness?" This iconic image of Uncle Sam first appeared on this cover of *Leslie's* before it became a U. S. Army recruitment poster in 1917. Reproduction. Artist: James Montgomery Flagg. 12" x 17.5"

Leslie's Illustrated Weekly Newspaper, March 29, 1917. Uncle Sam is bracketed by a U. S. Army soldier and a U. S. Navy sailor. Artist: Charles Sarka. 10.5" x 12"

Leslie's Illustrated Weekly Newspaper, May 10, 1917. The United States' National Symbol – the Bald Eagle – is perched atop the three flags of the Allies: United States, Great Britain, and France. Artist: Charles Sarka. 10.5" x 12"

Leslie's, December 29, 1917. An angry Uncle Sam is shown in the same iconic pose as the famous poster, but instead of pointing his finger Uncle Sam is pointing a gun and saying: "Get Off That Throne!" Artist: James Montgomery Flagg. 10.5" x 12"

Leslie's Illustrated Weekly Newspaper, January 5, 1918. "Three Speeds Forward and No Reverse!": Lady Columbia is driving a roadster while her partner, Uncle Sam, is vigilantly holding a rifle ready. The Bald eagle is flying cover. Artist: James Montgomery Flagg. 10.5" x 12"

Leslie's Illustrated Weekly Newspaper, January 28, 1918. "Allies": Uncle Sam with his Sorrel colored horse. Artist: James Montgomery Flagg. 10.5" x 12"

Liberty, January 19, 1935. Uncle Sam taking bows for the fact that domestic unemployment is receding during the Great Depression. The cover is a perfect image of twentieth century Americana and very rare. Reproduction cover; no artist named. 10.25" x 14.25"

While Uncle Sam was more and more portrayed as a strong and vigilant personification of America, in his place several artists use the image of a dog as a replacement for the better known caricature face. Typically the dog was white furred and resembled a feisty terrier.

A Great Dane (actually a German dog, the Deutsche Doggen) is standing over an American Bull Terrier, which is protecting a group of kittens hiding under an American flag. The captions reads "Safe: Under the Right Protection" and alludes to the United States' protection of England, France, and other European countries before and during World War I. The original artwork for the card was painted by artist Wallace Robinson in 1915. It was published by the Henry Heininger Co. of New York.

"Oh Boy! Can't he fight?" The American Bull Terrier, representing the United States with his patriotic collar and the American flag on the doghouse, reveal America's new sentiments about fighting to preserve liberty. Published by the Illustrated Postal Card & Novelty Co., 1917.

The American Bull Terrier, "America's Pride," exclaims, "My Hat's Not in the Ring" to other countries – English Bull, Russian Wolfhound, French Bull, German Dachshund, Austria-Hungary St. Bernard, and Italian Greyhound – as an indication of America's isolationist sentiment. Published by Schrader-Kellogg Co.

While James Montgomery Flagg painted many WWI patriotic posters, other artists contributed to the war's pictorial propaganda effort using vivid imagery to effect recruitment or the purchase of government bonds and savings stamps.

"It's Up To You … Protect The Nation's Honor … Enlist Now!" Associated Motion Picture Advertisers, 28" x 42". *Poster from the authors' private collection.*

"Keep Him free … Buy War Savings Stamps issued by the United States Treasury Dept." Artist: Charles Livingston Bull. 20" x 30". *Poster from the authors' private collection.*

"2nd Liberty Loan of 1917 (Buy a United States Government Bond)": "Shall we be more tender with our dollars than with the lives of our sons." Artist: Dan Sayre Groesbeck. 20" x 30". *Poster from the authors' private collection.*

"The Navy Needs You! Don't Read American History–MAKE IT!" U. S. Recruiting Station poster. Artist: James Montgomery Flagg. 28" x 42". *Poster from the authors' private collection.*

LIFE, May 23, 1918. "HELP! The Woman's Land Army of America": An appreciative Uncle Sam thanks a woman (a Gibson girl) who is using her gardening skills to provide food for domestic use "until the Boys come back." Artist: Charles Gibson Dana. Reproduction. 10.5" x 13"

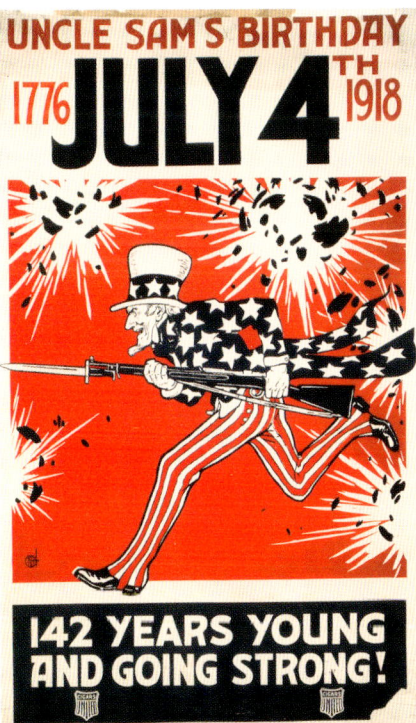

"Uncle Sam's Birthday 1776 JULY 4TH 1918 … 142 Years Young and Going Strong!": This reproduction poster depicts Uncle Sam running with his rifle at the ready through "bombs bursting in air." Artist unknown. 8" x 13"

American postcards just like patriotic music of World War I did not all have to be serious. Many portrayed the humorous rambunctiousness of the American "doughboy" during his duties as a soldier especially his plans for what he was going to do toward the German enemy. The war ended with an Allied victory and some of the leading cartoonists drew upon their thoughts.

"Keep the home-fires burning!" The young boy is doing his part in the war effort – burning all his toys that were "Made in Germany." Artist: D. Tempest. Published by Bamforth & Co., 1918.

"Say, Bill! My Hat's in the Ring." Uncle Sam now professes a new change of sentiment of the United States during World War I. He is in "the ring" and he is ready to do battle against the Kaiser. Artist: Bernhardt Wall. Publisher is unknown.

Uncle Sam is sounding his horn and is calling all recruits. This very young boy laments, "Gee! But I Wish I Was Growed Up!" Published by Shiloh Postcards.

Bernhardt Wall, born in 1872, was a Connecticut Yankee. He wintered in La Porte, Texas, his wife's family home, for many years. Bernhardt Wall was mainly an etcher who illustrated many books. In the mid-1930s he produced at least three books of copper-plate engravings during his annual Texas sojourns: *Following General Sam Houston, 1793-1863* (1935), *Following Stephen F. Austin, Father of Texas* (1936), and *Following Andrew Jackson* (1937). Wall is known for his Halloween postcards and his series of wide-eyed children's series "Sunbonnet Babies." During the First World War, Bernhardt Wall designed a large number of patriotic comic postcards, "mocking" Germany. Slogans on the cards say it all! Publisher is unknown.

The Independent, November 23, 1918. Cartoon Comment "The War Thus Comes To An End" shows a series of six cartoons drawn from the pages of leading newspapers. 8" x 11.5".

The Independent. Close-up of previous image shows a stern but relieved Uncle Sam saying "Thank God!" while holding a newspaper with the message: "The War Is Over!"

"Slam the Axis" postcard series:
Published by D. Robbins & Co., 1943

Fortune Teller (Uncle Sam): "I see a bad finish for you rats." This card shows the three Axis leaders depicted as rats at the fortune teller's booth as the "fortune teller" predicts their defeat.

Uncle Sam, with his rifle and bayonet, is running Hitler off with the caption: "Adolf's Going Places! ... To Hell."

Three Axis leaders – Hitler, Mussolini, and Tojo – are hanging from a particularly formed tree. Tojo is hanging from a branch shaped like the "rising sun" while Hitler and Mussolini are hanging from a swastika shaped branch.

General MacArthur called the Women's Army Corps (WACs) "my best soldiers," adding that they worked harder, complained less, and were better disciplined than men. Many generals wanted more of them and proposed to draft women, but it was realized that this "would provoke considerable public outcry and Congressional opposition" so the War Department declined to take such a drastic measure. Those 150,000 women that voluntarily did serve released the equivalent of seven divisions of men for combat. Gen. Dwight D. Eisenhower said that "their contributions in efficiency, skill, spirit, and determination are immeasurable." Two cards that give importance to the Women's Army Corps: (1) "Don't worry … Uncle Sam is keeping us in line"; and (2) Two WACs pounce on Hitler… "Our Country did it before and we are going to help do it again!" Publisher: Beals, Des Moines, Iowa.

"V" is for Victory. Uncle Sam, rolling up his shirt sleeves, asks us to be, at all times, ready to "Defend Your Country." Published by Tichnor Bros.; "Victory" Series, 1941.

Uncle Sam, filled with fury, spanks a Japanese child as the personification of Japan; the child is crying as a result. Uncle Sam wants all to know (and never forget): "Remember Pearl Harbor!" Artist signed Paris. Published by E. C. Kropp Co.

The New Yorker, July 1, 1950.
Artist: W. Cotton.

The New Yorker, July 4, 1970.
Artist: Charles Addams.

The New Yorker, January 3, 1977.
Artist: Stevenson.

The New Yorker, July 4, 1988.
Artist: Lee Lorenz.

The New Yorker, July 6, 1998.
Artist: Edward Sorel.

Pictorial Images of Uncle Sam

From its inception *The New Yorker* magazine on an ad-hoc basis contracted with artists to paint images of various holidays, usually in a humorous format. Depending upon the whim of the publisher, there appeared to be no rhyme or reason when one holiday was selected to grace the front of the magazine. Years could go by without a particular holiday being featured. Likewise there was no mention of the holiday within the pages of *The New Yorker* to tie it to the cover. However, readers should be grateful to the publisher of *The New Yorker* because virtually no other American magazine today uses live artists to portray, at some expense, renditions of holidays without resorting to photographs. This could be said in its entirety as *The New Yorker* has used original illustrations for each of its covers week after week.

Citrus crate labels, due to their vividly colorful images, are a highly collectible form of art. Paper labels began to be used in the 1880s as a method to entice East Coast buyers to purchase their oranges over some other packers since oranges were a commodity item subject only to grading by size. Growers and packers utilized creative graphic artists to create their labels in order to call attention to their respective products in the face of hundreds of competitors. Crate labels were not only used for citrus fruit, but also for other types of fruits as well as vegetables. Patriotic crate labels from the 1920s and 1930s are a favorite of collectors.

Orange Crate label: "I Grow These Myself in California." Packed by Riverside Navel Orange Company, Riverside, California. Calvert Lith. Co, Detroit. Trademark November 8, 1896.

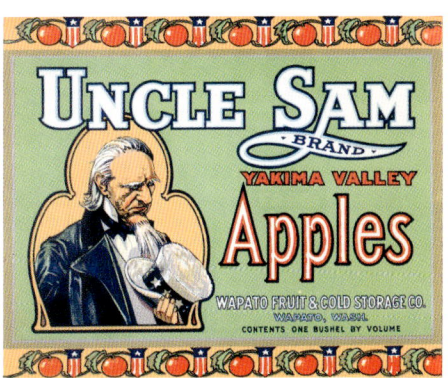

Crate Label: "Uncle Sam Brand" Yakima Valley Apples. Wapato Fruit and Cold Storage Co., Wapato, Washington. Green label, circa 1920s.

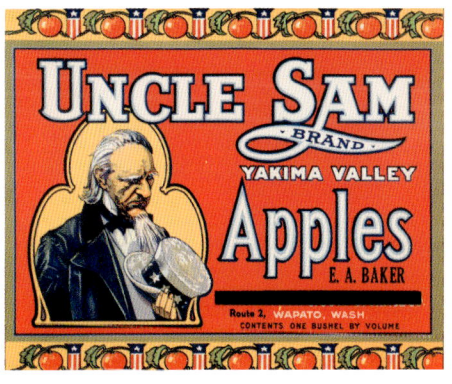

Crate Label: "Uncle Sam Brand," Yakima Valley Apples. Wapato, Washington. Red label, circa 1920s.

Orange Crate Label: "Old America." Packed by Pinkham and McKevitt, California, circa 1920s.

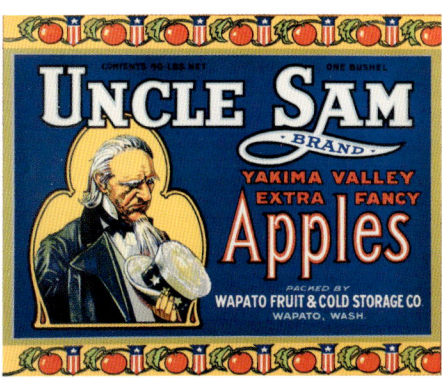

Crate Label: "Uncle Sam Brand," Yakima Valley Extra Fancy Apples. Wapato Fruit and Storage Co., Wapato, Washington. Blue label, circa 1920s.

Columbia and Lady Liberty

A kinder and gentler symbol of the national personification of America is the female allegorical figures of Columbia and Lady Liberty. Like Brother Jonathan and Uncle Sam who evolved at different times in our nation's history and were seen as different symbols, Columbia and Lady Liberty are also considered to be two separate American personifications. In the very earliest history of America, a Native American female, the "Indian Queen," was used to represent America. As the nation grew in sophistication, classical iconography changed the image of the rustic queen or princess into something more refined, resembling a Greek Goddess. Typically, Columbia and Lady Liberty were shown as youthful women wearing classically draped garments decorated with the iconic stars and stripes and a Phrygian cap of liberty. Their interchangeable costume included a red-and-white striped dress either flowing or form-fitted along with a blue blouse decorated with white stars. In many cases, however, the female allegories wore a white flowing dress as the embodiment of purity. Each of the figures usually were accompanied by props such as the Bald Eagle, Broken Chains, Cornucopia, Flag with Pole, Laurel Wreath, Liberty Pole and Hat, Olive Branch, Rattlesnake, Scales, and the Shield of the United States.

In the late 1800s, the concept of a dual identity of Columbia and Lady Liberty began to diverge. Originally the name Columbia was first used as a synonym for America by the British in 1738. The reference was somewhat obvious: Christopher Columbus discovered the New World and, therefore, Columbia was taken to mean the "Land of Columbia." At that time or a bit later, other countries came also to be represented by female allegorical figures using neoclassical names, such as "Britannia" for Great Britain; "Germania" for Germany; "Iberia" for Spain; "Italia Turrita" for Italy; and "Marianne" for France. While the personification of Columbia has since fallen out of use, she was considered to be a gentler version of Uncle Sam as a worldwide figure.

However, after the neoclassical, 151-foot Statue of Liberty was placed on Liberty Island in New York Harbor and dedicated on October 28, 1886, Lady Liberty or, alternatively, the Goddess of Liberty, began its ascent as the personification of America. She has come to be thought of as an internal symbol as America's mother comforting all of those who come here to escape tyranny while offering the ideals of freedom and opportunity. Today, Lady Liberty is an ever-present icon and the Statue of Liberty, which she represents, celebrated its 116th Anniversary in 2012.

On a side note: While not strictly a personification, certain "nurses" images were depicted to be symbols of comfort, service, and care for the war wounded.

Puck, January 29, 1890. Chromolithographic illustration "Better No Senate Than A Boodle Senate": Columbia has a pained look about her as she wholeheartedly dumps the "senators" into a basket with a sign "For Political Waste." The allegorical message is that during the Harrison Administration many senators were accused of being "bought" for their votes. Boodle means accepting a bribe for money. So Columbia, in a house cleaning, closed the Senate down for "fumigation" purposes. Out with the old and in with the new!

Puck, early 1900s. Chromolithographic illustration "In Danger": Lady Liberty, as the embodiment of domestic affairs, is horrified at the sight of a very large green snake – "Monopoly" – and its hold on the White House with its tail securely wrapped around the Dome. In the background Puck asks Uncle Sam, "What are you going to do about it?" Toward the end of "The Gilded Age" (1865-1900) of economic prosperity in the United States, many tycoons amassed vast financial empires, of which a majority came about due to restraint of trade, i.e, "monopolies." Because of this wealth, business interests acquired significant influence over the government. The steel, oil, and railroad monopolies controlled the economy of America until the Progressives took over after the 1900s with the result that laws were passed to regulate businesses and ensure competition and free enterprise.

"Sow the Seeds of Victory! Every Garden a Munition Plant!" Artist: James Montgomery Flagg. 22" x 33". *Poster is from the author's private collection.*

Columbia wears a laurel wreath while carrying the American flag as well as a bouquet of red, white, and blue flowers. This impressive card is enhanced by stars and flags. Publisher is unknown.

Crate label: "Columbia Belle." Two Quality Washington State Apples labels feature Columbia, one with a blue background and one with red. Columbia Fruit Distributors, Wenatchee, Washington, c. 1920s.

Columbia is draped in the flag and holds the Declaration of Independence in one hand and a shield with the eagle in the other. She is wearing a laurel wreath with an olive branch at her side. The Liberty Bell protects them all. "The Liberty we claimed in 1776 is the same we enjoy today." Publisher is unknown.

"Miss Liberty" at sunrise with sparklers in her hand – "At Dawn's first peep, awakes the echoes from their sleep"; and at the end of the day, the dark sky is lit up with her vivid flares – "Quite debonair, ends the day with rocket's flare." Published by The Photo-color-graph Co., New York; a four-card series entitled "Dawn," "Noon," "Sunset," and "Night."

Columbia is wrapped in the colorful flag holding the Scales of Justice in one hand and the Columbia Shield in the other hand. She is standing on a radiant star. A gold scroll encircles the image. Postcard is embossed with gold highlights. Published by L. R. Conwell; No. 387, c. 1910.

"Greetings from a Patriot." Columbia, dressed in her red, white, and blue robe decorated with stars, holds the Scales of Justice and an Olive Branch, the symbol for the offering of peace. Ribbons decorate the image; postcard embossed with gold highlights. Published by Nash; Series J-8.

Columbia, in her white flowing gown and wearing a Phrygian cap, proudly holds the flag and sword. "Columbia Calls," a poem by Frances Adams Halsted, is written at the bottom of the card. Two of the verses are: "Awake! Ye men from dreams of Peace – Nor sleep when danger's near, But fling Old Glory to the breeze–There are no cowards here! Our fathers fought; Like heroes died, for years their blood they gave That honor, home and Peace be ours: Awake! Thy country save!" Publisher is unknown.

Lady Liberty remembers the veterans of the Civil War. "Honor the Brave! 1861-1865." She is dressed in a flowing white gown while holding the flag of our country. The Statue of Liberty in the background reminds us of our freedom and liberties. Published by the Illustrated Postal Card Co., c. 1907.

The Statue of Liberty shines brightly with a rising sun as Uncle Sam metaphorically welcomes immigrants by opening the star-studded curtain. Published by the Illustrated Postal Cards Co.

A young boy portraying a wounded soldier and the young girl dressed as the "Red Cross Nurse" emphasizes the importance of the Red Cross in the history of the wars. Published by A. M. Davis & Co., London; "Khaki Kiddies" Series No. 514.

The American Red Cross was established by Clara Barton, who was dubbed "Angel of the Battlefield," as she began giving aid to servicemen in the American Civil War. This postcard illustrates the work of the Red Cross in France. The Red Cross established the Nurse's Aide program to make up for the shortage of nurses during World War I. "Somewhere in France" a nurse is coming to the aid of the soldiers. Published by Anglo-American Publishing Co., it was distributed by the American Red Cross in France.

The iconic symbols of Uncle Sam and Columbia were so popular during the heydays of postcards that their images were successfully used in the postcards of other holidays such as Christmas, Thanksgiving, and St. Patrick's Day.

St. Patrick's Day is celebrated. Card No.1: Uncle Sam and a red-haired Irish Colleen kiss. The two figures are enhanced by the bright gold metallic background. Published by Barton Spooner; Series No. 7041. Card No.2: Uncle Sam holds a shillelagh and the Irish and American flags. There is also a "Wishing you Luck" horseshoe. Publisher is unknown.

Christmas is celebrated. Uncle Sam and Santa Claus greet each other as Santa raises his glass in a toast to Uncle Sam over a holly branch. Publisher is unknown; "Xmas-Santa Claus" Series.

Thanksgiving is celebrated. Card No.1: Uncle Sam carries a turkey getting ready for the kill (S.B. Series No. 259); Card No.2: Miss Liberty, dressed in her red, white, and blue gown, walks along two tom turkeys with a gilded background of stars (Publisher is unknown; Series No. 208); Card No.3: Uncle Sam proudly serves the turkey to his guests enhanced by decorative ribbons (A & S publisher); Card No.4: Surrounded by a border of gold stars, Uncle Sam, with his bib tucked in, is served his Thanksgiving meal with cranberries and wine added to the menu (A & S publisher).

Celebrating

America's Patriotism

Section Two

Chapter 3

Independence Day

A National Day is a designated date on which celebrations mark the nationhood of a sovereign country. In the case of the United States, during the initial stages of the American Revolutionary War, the Second Continental Congress voted to approve a resolution of independence declaring the United States independent from Great Britain. This resolution, which created a legal separation of the thirteen colonies from Great Britain, occurred on July 2, 1776. A document that explained the decision to vote for independence, called the Declaration of Independence, was primarily authored by Thomas Jefferson. After two days of debate and revisions, the Continental Congress approved the final official document on July 4, 1776. The Declaration of Independence was then signed by the fifty-six delegates to the Continental Congress by August 2, 1776.

When the Declaration of Independence was first approved, the unsigned version was immediately sent to a printer for publication and, as a broadside, distributed locally to governmental agencies and several Commanding Officers of the Continental Army. The first newspaper to print the entire text of the Declaration was the *Pennsylvania Evening Post* on July 6th and, by July 8th, it had been read publicly in other adjacent locales. It was these public "proclamations" that constituted the first documented annual celebration of independence known as the Fourth of July. Once the Declaration was officially signed, Congress made sure that all thirteen states would have access to an authenticated copy by ordering a special printing of the signed document on January 18, 1777. The Declaration with which everyone is familiar is the authenticated copy.

While the text of the Declaration can be broken into five parts, the best known and widely quoted is the Preamble which, in part, embodies the principles contained to wit:

We hold these truths to be self-evident, that all men are created equal, that they are endowed by their Creator with certain inalienable Rights, among these are Life, Liberty and the pursuit of Happiness. That to secure these rights,

Governments are instituted among Men, deriving their just powers from the consent of the governed, That whenever any Form of Government becomes destructive of these ends, it is the Right of the People to alter or to abolish it, and to institute new Government…

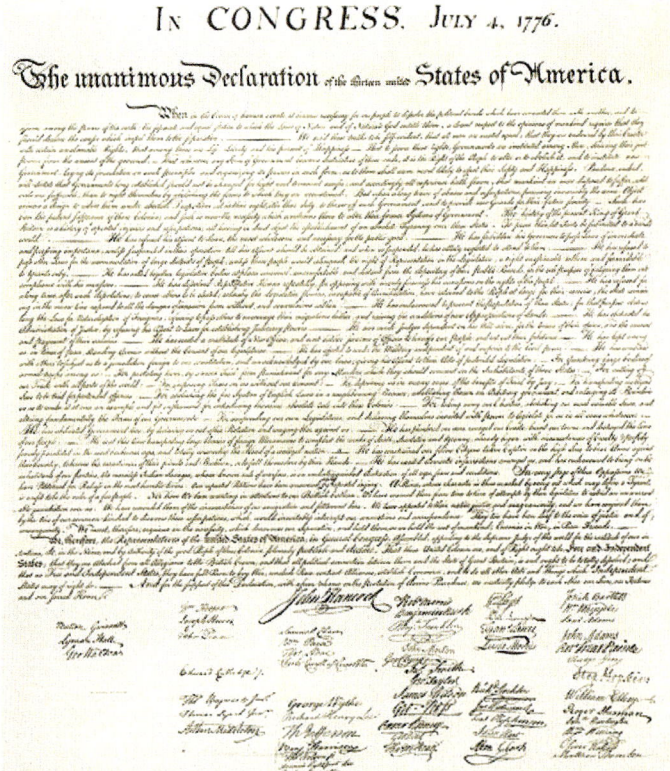

United States Declaration of Independence, July 4, 1776. This is an 1823 facsimile of the engraved copy.

The United States Congress adopts and signs the American Constitution on September, 17, 1787.

Since those words were first drafted and amended, they have served as a hallmark document for all future generations of man who aspire to be governed under democratic principles.

The high and moral principles of the Declaration of Independence does not a government make. After declaring independence, the next step for the Second Continental Congress was to draw up an agreement among the original thirteen states that legally established the United States of America as a confederation of sovereign states. This agreement, termed the Articles of Confederation, would serve as the first constitution. From the initial drafting stage in 1776 until the final formal ratification by all thirteen states on March 1, 1781, the Second Continental Congress acted as a provisional government in all forms of domestic and foreign relations especially since the newly independent country was still at war with Great Britain. The first Article out of thirteen established the name of the new confederation as "The United States of America."

After The Treaty of Paris in 1783 in which the British Government recognized the sovereignty of the United States, there was recognition among many in Congress that, due to the increasing size and complexity of America, a strong central Federal government was needed, especially to raise revenues from taxes, which, in part, would be used to maintain a standing army. Therefore, in May 1787 the U. S. Constitution Convention delegates met in Philadelphia to design a radically new form of government that included a bicameral Congress, a judiciary, and a President as Chief Executive. From May to September the fifty-five delegates hammered out the tenants of the American Constitution, which was created on September 17, 1787. That date today is called Constitution Day. The United States Constitution was ratified on June 21,

Actual photo of the Independence Day parade with Lady Liberty, Uncle Sam, and a World War I (Red Cross) Nurse leading the way, New York City, 1919.

1788, by the last of twelve states. The Constitution is the supreme law of America. The first ten amendments to the Constitution are known as the Bill of Rights, which guarantees a range of personal freedoms and legal protections; it was adopted on August 21, 1789, and ratified on December 15, 1791.

Independence Day, commonly called the Fourth of July, was first annually commemorated in Philadelphia on July 4, 1777. In 1781, Massachusetts became the first state to declare July 4th an official state celebration, and in 1791, the first recorded use of the name "Independence Day" occurred. Beginning in 1795, Bristol, Rhode Island, has hosted the oldest continuous Independence Day celebration with its

Bristol Fourth of July parade. On June 28, 1870, the United States Congress first declared the Fourth Day of July (Independence Day) as a Federal holiday, although unpaid for federal employees. Finally, on June 29, 1938, by a joint resolution of the U. S. Congress, the Fourth of July was legislatively changed to a paid Federal holiday. Over time the Federal holiday known originally as the Fourth of July became to be known officially as Independence Day. Also, while there are Federal holidays (ten annually plus one every four years) as designated by the U. S. Congress in Title V of the United States Code, there are no national holidays because Congress only has authority to mandate holidays for federal institutions. Obviously, as most state holidays concur with Federal holidays, governmental offices are closed along with most financial institutions, but private enterprises may opt to stay open and can do so legally.

In a letter to his wife dated July 5, 1776, John Adams wrote, "The second day of July, 1776, will be the most memorable epoch in the history of America… It ought to be solemnized with pomp and parade, with shows, games, sports, guns, bells, bonfires, and illuminations…" Throw in some John Philip Sousa style-patriotic concerts, fireworks, flag flying, family reunions, picnics, and barbecues, and John Adams would be prescient in stating that Independence Day "will be celebrated by succeeding generations as the great anniversary festival."

4th of July in Postcards

From the turn-of-the-nineteenth century into early twentieth century, postcards were an extremely inexpensive form of communication. The postal rate was 1¢ from July 1, 1898, to November 2, 1917, after which it increased to 2¢ due to the war tax. The vivid palette of postcards changed seasonally to reflect the "natural" colors invocative of any greetings particularly holidays. Fourth of July postcards were especially bright and colorful due to the interaction of red, white, blue, and yellow colors. While many themes were portrayed on the cards, some images appear over and over again such as the Statue of Liberty, Uncle Sam, Lady Liberty, the Bald Eagle, fireworks, American Patriots, and children. The following images reflect these themes.

A vivid blue border sets off the golden Statue of Liberty. Artist signed Bernhardt Wall. Published by Ullman Manufacturing Co.; "Independence Day" Series 122.

Flags and eagle along with the American flag provide the festive background for the Statue. Published by GDD (Gottschalk, Greyfuss, and Davis); Series 2172.

The Statue of Liberty shines in the rays of the rising sun. Published by PFB (Paul Finkenrath); Series 8252.

A circle of golden stars surrounds the golden Statue. Publisher is unknown; Series No. 420.

A simple but magnificent image of Uncle Sam enveloped by the smoke of the firecrackers. Published by Winsch.

Uncle Sam proudly showing the Declaration of Independence to the world. Publisher is unknown; Series 752.

Uncle Sam is surrounded by all the icons of the 4th of July: the Bald eagle, firecrackers, flags, and cannon. The publisher is unknown; Series H3028.

Uncle Sam "shoots" out of a firecracker while celebrating the holiday. The publisher is unknown.

An eagle and a golden banner decorate this card. The message "4th of July" is scripted using firecrackers. Publisher is unknown.

Standing on a cannon Uncle Sam proclaims, "Give us Independence." Published by PFB (Paul Finkenrath); Series 8252.

Uncle Sam holds the talons of the eagle as firecrackers pop in the background. Publisher is unknown.

Uncle Sam takes center stage surrounded by red, white, and blue ribbons and rockets. Published by E. Nash; Series J-8.

A vivid blue background sets off Uncle Sam holding the American flag. Artist signed Bernhardt Wall. Published by Ullman Manufacturing Co.; "Independence Day" Series 122.

Uncle Sam is all smiles dancing on "top of the world" celebrating his birthday. Artist signed G. Howard Hilder. Published by Osborne Ltd.

Uncle Sam leaps over a burning rocket as he proclaims, "Hurrah for the Fourth of July." Published by S. B.; Series 258.

Uncle Sam holds a flag decorated with "July 4" written in pink roses. Published by GDD (Gottschalk, Dreyfuss, and Davis); Series 2099.

Uncle Sam is propelled into space aboard a shooting rocket. Published by PBF (Paul Finkenrath); Series 9507.

A vivid blue border sets off Miss Independence draped with an American flag. Artist signed Bernhardt Wall. Published by Ullman Manufacturing Co.; "Independence Day" Series 122.

Columbia is brightened by the sun's ray as she is adorned by the flag and laurel branches. Publisher is unknown.

"A pair that's hard to beat": Miss Liberty holds on to the eagle protected by the shield. Publisher is unknown.

Miss Liberty, floating between the wings of the Bald Eagle, raises the flag. Publisher is unknown; Series H3028.

"Teach him to hold the flag holy and high...": Sparkling firecrackers brighten Miss Liberty. Published by Tuck & Sons; "Independence Day" Series No. 109.

A Liberty Bell and Eagle adorn Miss Liberty with "4th of July" written in firecracker script. Publisher is unknown.

Two young children with innocent and angelic faces play the part of Uncle Sam and Lady Columbia. Publisher is unknown (artwork attributed to Ellen Clapsaddle).

A border of flags and eagles accent Uncle Sam and Miss Liberty with the Capitol and the eagle in the background. Published by GDD; Series 2172.

"Hurrah for the Fourth of July": Uncle Sam and Miss Liberty introduce themselves and then walk together in celebration. Publisher is unknown; Series 753.

Uncle Sam kisses the hand of Lady Columbia. Published by S. B.; Series 258.

Uncle Sam takes a rocket from the armful of Miss Liberty as they greet each other. Published by Santway; Series 129.

Two postcards that welcome and offer freedom to the Native American nations and also to those coming to the United States in hope of a better life. Publisher is unknown.

A starry night envelopes the eagle as he watches over the world. Published by P. Sander.

The Bald Eagle takes center stage surrounded by popping fireworks. Published by S. B.; Series 258.

An embossed eagle holds a laurel wreath over the Revolutionary troops symbolizing victory. Published by J. J. Marks; "4th July Series" Number 706.

A Bald Eagle sits on a cannon as it shoots out the 4th of July greeting. Publisher is unknown.

The eagle is the dominant image sitting upon two firecrackers. Published by Winsch.

"I will go off with you on the 4th!" says the young lady, holing onto a gigantic firecracker. She is clearly ready to celebrate. The publisher is unknown; "4th July" Series No. 705.

"I see my finish on the 4th!" declares the shooting rocket. Published by Julius Bien & Co.; Series 7003.

Not only is this a very colorful card, it is also a "fold-down" card (right) that surprises the reader as he opens it. The signer of the Declaration of Independence shoots into the air as the mischievous boys light the rocket. Publisher is unknown; Copyright H 152.

Collier's The National Weekly, July 6, 1907. The wick of a large firecracker, which the children are exuberantly using as a Maypole, has just been lit. Artist: Walter Jack Duncan. 10" x 14"

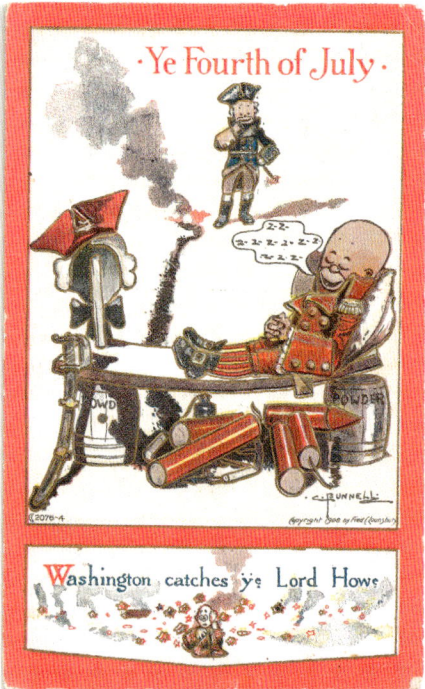

Firecrackers not only scare the two surprised boys, but also frighten the dogs. Artist signed W.S.D. Published by the Valentine & Sons' Publishing Co.

A comical spin on the battles with Lord Howe, one of the outstanding leaders of the British government, and the Battle of Princeton. Artist signed C. Bunnell. Postcards published by Fred Lounsbury.

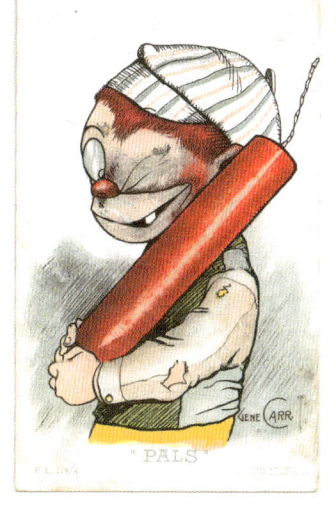

United States cartoonist Gene Carr (January 1881 – December 1959) was one of the most active early New York City artists in the young field of comic strips. He was doing newspaper cartoons by age fifteen; two years later, he was working for the William Randolph Hearst newspapers. Comical series No. 219, a set of six postcards, picture bumptious dogs and nasty little children, loaded with their firecrackers, preparing to play jokes on both the dog ("Nice dorg!") and the gentleman ("What are you laughing at?"). The celebration ends on the 5th of July, with a young boy bandaged from head to toe pictured with a crutch, witch hazel, and liniment for his wounds; however the dog is raring to celebrate again! Artist signed Gene Carr. Published by The Rotograph Company. Circa early 1900s.

A cartoon showing the frightened faces of the children as they play with firecrackers. Note the bulldog in the background waiting for action. Publisher is unknown.

A group of comical postcards each lamenting the tragic results of a gun or firecracker accident: "Johnny had a brand new gun…which leg to amputate."; "Paul found a musket…loaded it with powder, 'twas the end of Paul." "Little fellow…held a cannon cracker in his hand, has gone to join the Angel's Band." Artist signed WH. Published by The Rose Company.

Three cards from a comical set of six, each with very funny quotes: "Fotograph your boy before the 4th of July; you may not get a chance after" … as the rocket explodes close to the boy and his dog. Or "How to prevent your boy being killed on the Fourth of July … kill him on the Third" laugh his parents. Or "Where ignorance is bliss tis folly to be wise" as two men have an innocent conversation not realizing what the two boys are planning. Publisher is unknown; "Fourth of July" Series No. 1.

Each card in the series is bordered by red, blue, and white ribbons along with firecrackers and contain a very celebrated image in the center: George Washington, Uncle Sam, a soldier from the Revolutionary War, and Lady Liberty. Published by E. Nash.

Thomas Jefferson is proudly handing the Declaration of Independence to Uncle Sam. A young girl in her dress decorated with golden glitter holds firecrackers in one hand and the flag in the other while a young sailor pretends to load the cannon, both wishing "Fourth of July Greetings." Publisher is unknown; Series 752.

All ages celebrate the 4th: Young boys dressed as sailors parade as the girl in a fancy red dress and flowery hat watch (note the doll in her hand) while a woman, proudly carrying a flag, walks on the waterfront possibly thinking about sailors at sea. Publisher is unknown.

Celebrating the 4th: A young lady waves her lighted sparklers; a young sailor boy lights his firecrackers; a solder raises the flag as he shoots his gun; and a young boy fires a toy pistol at his cat. Published by PFB (Paul Finkenrath); Series No. 8252.

Firecrackers, sparklers, cannons, and drums decorate these postcards focusing on three young children all ready to celebrate. Published by P. Sander; Series No. 440.

Children dressed in a variety of uniforms come together for "United We Stand"; children gather on the seashore proudly waving their flags; and a veteran plays "Yankee Doodle" while a young boy "rides on a pony." Red, white, and blue stripes set off the images. Artist signed C. Chapman. Published by S. Garre; Series No. 51668.

A throng of young boys celebrating the holiday, marching in a parade, or waving sparklers over a balcony. Notice the card that includes a black friend, which is rarely pictured in July 4th postcards. Also note that the celebration appears to have gotten out of hand with a bonfire quickly growing. Publisher unknown. Series No. 746

With a fireworks display all around, two boys dance in celebration. Artist signed G. Howard Hilder. Published by Osborne Ltd.

Two children, one dressed as George Washington and one as a sailor, shoot a gun or rocket through the gold metallic looking glass to write out "4th of July." Eagles, cannons, and colorful ribbons decorate the cards. Published by P. Sander.

Various scenes of the celebration are all highlighted by a red, white, and blue striped border, but each card contains a very patriotic wish: "May you always be satisfied with the proudest title a man can wear: An American Citizen"; "May the hiss of the Rocket…and the sight of the Stars and Stripes ever continue to thrill you and make you feel proud"; "May you never be too old to…sing My Country Tis of Thee…"; "May your heart ever be thrilled at the sight of the glorious Star Spangled Banner…"; "May Old Glory always be the first sight to your eye…"; and "May you have a rip roaring Old Star Spangled Fourth of July with no after effects." Publisher is unknown; "Fourth of July" Series No 2.

A gold or silver metallic background encompasses the images on these cards. Children dressed in their red, white, and blue take part in all types of activities: Waving the flags, playing the drums, and shooting off fireworks to celebrate the holiday. Publisher is unknown (attributed to Nash); "Fourth of July" Series No. 3.

Playful girls dressed in their sweet dresses trimmed with colorful ribbons and some of the boys in sailor uniforms all get ready to celebrate the 4th. Stars abound on the cards. Publisher is unknown (attributed to Nash); "Fourth of July Series" No. 4.

"Wishing you a Glorious 4th of July" appears on all six cards in this series. Children celebrate the 4th in all types of antics: lighting a cannon and pretending to shoot toy soldiers, trying to retrieve a firecracker from the mouth of their pet dog, carefully lighting a firecracker as friends hide and watch. Cards are bordered by gold and are decorated with gold stars. Published by E. Nash; "Fourth of July" Series No. 5.

Ellen Clapsaddle is known for her drawings of children who were accurate reflections of the times. The children on Clapsaddle cards are described by many as charming, delightful, and the picture of innocence. Clapsaddle was the most prolific of all American postcard artists, producing thousands of images for many holidays. Artist signed Ellen Clapsaddle. Published by International Art Publishing Company.

A vivid display of blasting fireworks and shooting cannons. Boys with their guns in their belts or carrying an arm-full of rockets and girls dressed fancily or as cowgirls abound in these colorful cards. Note that the same children appear over and over again on different cards. Published by P. Sander; Series 332.

"4th of July," written with firecrackers, headline the colorful cards. Even Uncle Sam joins the children on two of the cards. Note the faces of the children along with the cannons and flags. Published by Santway; Series No. 129.

Children dressed as a sailor, Uncle Sam, and George Washington are all ready for the 4th. Published by Tuck & Sons; "Independence Day" Series No. 109.

A father with his gun and a young girl with her flag parade in celebration of the 4th of July. Published by S. B.; Series 258.

Chapter 4

President's Day

Happy Birthday, George & Abe!

A Federal holiday in the United States is a public holiday recognized by the United States Government. There are eleven U. S. federal holidays, all of which are celebrated by the states. However, not every state recognizes each federal holiday. In 1870, the U. S. Government first recognized federal holidays with time off, but federal employees were not paid. These were New Year's Day, the Fourth of July, and Christmas Day. In 1880, the U. S. Government declared a federal holiday honoring George Washington, but only for the District of Columbia. In 1885, the celebration was extended to all federal offices across the country and the day chosen was Washington's actual birthday, February 22nd.

In 1951, there was a well-intentioned attempt to create a Presidents Day specifically not to honor any particular President but to honor the Office of the President. Not only did this bill languish for lack of interest, but a draft of the Uniform Monday Holiday Act also did not attract much support that would have renamed the holiday Presidents' Day to honor the birthdays of both Washington and Abraham Lincoln. However, in January 1971, due to the Uniform Monday Holiday Act, WASHINGTON'S BIRTHDAY was shifted to the third Monday in February. Therefore, Washington's birthday is a U. S. Federal holiday celebrated on the third Monday of February. On the other hand, Lincoln's birthday, February 12th, was never selected to be a federal holiday. In the mid-1980s advertisers began to promote "President's Day" sales and other activities. President's Day is now so much in the public's persona that the sobriquet has become the "unofficial" name for Washington's birthday. For purposes of this book, we celebrate the activities of both Presidents.

George Washington

February 22, 1732 – December 14, 1799

Washington was universally acclaimed as the "Father of his Country." He was not only the first President of the newly freed United States of America, but he was also considered to be its very best President with his legacy lasting over 220 years. Upon Washington's death, the now famous words of his eulogy ring true to his enduring character:

> *"First in war-first in peace-and first in the hearts of his countrymen, he was second to none in the humble and enduring scenes of private life…"*

Portrait of George Washington (The Athenaeum Portrait) by George Stuart, 1796. Publisher: Souvenir Post Card Co., New York. Printed in Germany, c. 1910s.

Three outstanding cards praising Washington as the country's leader: "First in war, First in Peace, First in the hearts of his Countrymen" (Series No. 51896); "First in the Hearts of his Countrymen" and "Three Cheers for George Washington" (Series No. 16250). Artist signed Ellen Clapsaddle. Published by International Art Publishing Company.

Highlights of Washington's Life

• Born into a relatively well-off Colonial Virginia family who had extensive tobacco interests in 1732 at Bridges Creek, Virginia.

• In 1749, he was appointed an official surveyor in a county in Virginia for the lands of Lord Fairfax.

• In the French & Indian Wars (1754-1758), Washington was eventually given the rank of Colonel of the Virginia Regiment, the first full-time military unit in the colonies; the Virginia Regiment were engaged in many pitched battles culminating with the capture of Fort Duquesne by a combined force of British regulars and colonial militiamen.

"Father of the Land We Love" song sheet. Lyrics and music by George M. Cohan; written for the American People to Commemorate the Two Hundredth Anniversary of the Birth of George Washington. Front sheet graphics based on the painting by James Montgomery Flagg: "First in War, First in Peace, First in the Hearts of his countrymen, That is the story of Washington, That is the glory of Washington, His spirit is here…" Original. 1932.

Washington as a Surveyor and at Fort Duquesne in 1758. Published by Tuck & Sons; "George Washington Birthday" Series No. 124.

Two views of Washington and his wife Martha: Two oval framed photos with a draped flag in the background (Published by H.I.R.; No. 329) and George Washington and Martha dressed in their finery (Publisher is unknown; "Washington Birthday" Series No. 1).

• Washington retired from his army commission in 1759, whereupon he married Martha Dandridge Curtis and they moved to their estate at Mount Vernon, Virginia. For the next fifteen years he expanded his estate at Mount Vernon, where he was a successful planter of tobacco and wheat.

• By 1775, Washington was becoming more politically active in the affairs of the Virginia colony. After the opening shots of the American Revolutionary War were fired at Lexington and Concord in April 1775 against British troops, Washington appeared at the Second Continental Congress to offer his military experience and service.

• Congress created the Continental Army in June 1775 and appointed Washington major-general and Commander-in-Chief. Over the course of six years of war with Great Britain, Washington's troops won important victories at Trenton, Saratoga, and culminated with the final British defeat at Yorktown in 1781, aided by French naval and ground forces. Prior to the victory at Yorktown, France conducted a treaty with the United States in March 1778, thus formally recognizing America as an independent country. This allowed France, through the help of Generals Lafayette and Rochambeau, to aid America with much needed men and capital. With the victories came defeats, such as the loss of New York City, Philadelphia, and the ports of Savannah and Charlestown.

"Washington – as General": Washington's image is featured on a golden axe with cherries as he leads the Revolutionary Army. Published by Nash; Series No. 6.

Crate Labels: "Martha Washington" and "Geo. Washington." Tustin Hills Citrus Assn., Tustin, California, c. 1920s.

• The very favorable public persona of Washington through American and British eyes took on an added allure through his famous crossing of the Delaware River in the dead of winter on the way to the Battle of Trenton and his courageous care and treatment of his men at his army's winter quarters at Valley Forge in 1777/1778.

• With the signing of the Treaty of Paris in September 1783, the British evacuated New York City within two months' time. In November, Washington disbanded the Continental Army, and in December he officially bade farewell to his officers and resigned his commission as Commander-in-Chief.

Two images of Washington as General: The red, white, and blue background is an artist signed Ellen Clapsaddle (Series No. 51896) and the Washington with a gold border is unsigned (Series No. 51646). Both images were published by the International Art Publishing Co. Often Washington is pictured on his white horse. During the Revolutionary War, Washington rode two horses at least, though there may have been others. His favorite mount, especially in time of action, was Nelson, a sorrel. The other horse was named Blue Skin. The latter horse seems to have been a light bluish gray, closely akin to white.

- From 1784 to 1787, Washington returned to Mount Vernon, where he renewed his role as a gentleman planter. In 1784, General Lafayette returned to the United States and visited Washington at Mt. Vernon. Due to Lafayette's good works in America during his visit, he was made a "natural born citizen" of the United States. In the summer of 1787, Washington went to Philadelphia for the Continental Convention, was elected President, and used his reputation to convince the members of the Thirteen States to ratify the newly written Constitution.
- The Electoral College voted unanimously for Washington to become the first President of the United States of America in 1789, whereupon he took the oath of office on April 30th in New York City. Washington was again unanimously elected to return as President in 1792, and he finished out his second full term of office in 1797. As First President of the United States, he started this country on her career as one of the greatest nations in all history.
- After retiring from the Presidency, Washington returned to Mount Vernon to resume his life as a planter/farmer and to produce his first batch of whiskey from his distillery. He was also brought back to the Government as a senior military officer to oversee plans for raising a provisional army for use in a potential war against France.
- When Washington again returned to the Mount Vernon estate, which was George and Martha's home for forty years, he encountered a respiratory disease that caused his death at the age of sixty-seven on December 14, 1799. His funeral was held December

Washington leads his troops across the Delaware River (Publisher is unknown) and Washington at Valley Forge (Published by L & E; Series No. 2228).

Washington as President of the United States. Publisher is unknown; "Washington Birthday" Series No. 1.

Washington greets Lafayette at Mount Vernon as Martha looks on. A blue border with golden eagles and stars highlight the card. Published by Tuck & Sons; "George Washington" Series No. 171.

Washington is pictured with his home, Mt. Vernon. Published by Nash; Series No. 11.

Copy of the painting of George Washington by Gilbert Stuart that hangs in the Museum of Fine Arts in Boston, Massachusetts. Published by Detroit Publishing Co.

Crate Label: "President." Frances Citrus Association, Tustin, California, c. 1919.

18th and he was interred at Mount Vernon. His final resting place was a new tomb authorized by Congress, and built on October 7, 1837, at Mount Vernon.

• A covenant in Washington's will stipulated that all of his slaves would be freed upon Martha's death, but she freed them twelve months after his death.

• Two presumably apocryphal stories persist about Washington in his youth: (1) He skipped a silver dollar across the Potomac River at Mount Vernon; and (2) He chopped down his father's cherry tree with a small hatchet and forthrightly admitted to the deed. Nothing can be proven or disproven so the stories remain as a mainstay of Washington's reputation. However, closely associated with many images of Washington are bright red cherries.

George Washington was a man of many fine personal characteristics and traits — qualities that stood him well both as a Commander-in-Chief and President. It is very appropriate that Washington's Birthday was selected as one of the very first Federal patriotic holidays that our country celebrates.

"Let us raise a standard to which the wise and the honest can repair." The American flag provides the background for Washington's portrait. Published by The Rotograph Co.; Series 225.

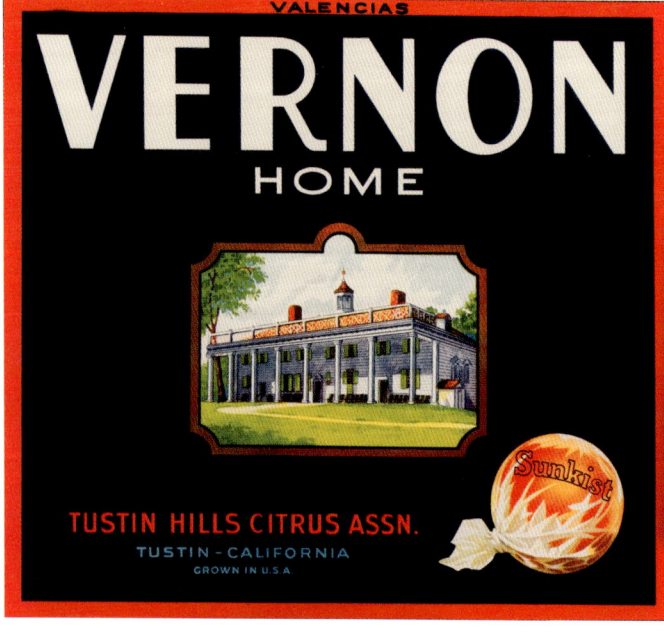

Crate Labels: "Vernon Home" and "Martha Washington." Tustin Hills Citrus Assn., Tustin, California, c. 1920s.

Three postcards (from a series of six) that highlight the life of Washington. Surrounded by a garland of pink and red roses, Washington is remembered for his famous speeches, one being: "The name America must always exalt the just pride of patriotism." Publisher is unknown.

Washington, as a young boy, states "Father, I cannot tell a lie, I did it with my Little Hatchet" about the legend that he cut down his father's beloved cherry tree. Publisher is unknown; "Washington Birthday" Series No. 1.

Washington's portrait in the gold frame is surrounded by red, white, and blue ribbons and gold stars. Published by Winsch.

129

Two images appear on this postcard: Little George Washington is pictured with his hatchet with the broken tree in the background; Washington as President "First in peace, first in war, and first in the hearts of his countrymen. Publisher is unknown; Series No. 540.

"Here's to the hatchet which holds a high place, Forever distinguished by fame!" The famous hatchet is decorated by ribbons and brightly colored cherries. Published by International Art Publishing Co.; Series No. 51646.

Cherries take center stage on these postcards. The cards with the deep blue background are part of Series No. 16250 and the image with the cherry tree in the ribbon decorated flower pot is Series No. 51896. Artist signed Ellen Clapsaddle. Published by International Art Publishing Company.

A comical postcard depicting George Washington's father's reaction to "Georgie never told a lie" while Little George muses "I guess the old man will be a good sport about this since I saw him kiss the cook today." Publisher is unknown.

A familiar portrait of George Washington is trimmed with red, white, and blue stars along with bright red cherries. Artist signed Ellen Clapsaddle. Published by International Art Publishing Co.

The shadowed image of George Washington is decorated by an axe, a flag, and a basket of cherries. A border of gold stars highlights the image. Published by Tuck & Sons; "Washington Birthday" Series No. 178

Replica of the hatchet that young George Washington reputedly used to cut down his father's cherry tree. Painted molded paper candy container with ribbon. 11.5" length x 5" wide. Made in Germany.

A sweet innocent child in his patched pants admires the small cherry tree that he has chopped down with his axe -- just like George Washington. Artist signed Ellen Clapsaddle. Published by International Art Publishing Co.

Six postcards, each enhanced by cherries, axes, silver stars, and the red, white, and blue, recognize the personal qualities of George Washington that led to his Presidency. Published by E. Nash; "Washington Birthday" Series No. 2.

These very collectible postcards honor George Washington with innocent children offering their adorations to him. Both cards are vividly colored in red, white, and blue. Artist signed Ellen Clapsaddle. Published by International Art Publishing Company; Series No. 16250.

A young lady offers a toast to George Washington in celebration of his birthday. Published by T. P. & Co.; Series No. 522.

A real celebration for Washington's Birthday with eagle, flag, and stars decorating his portrait. Publisher is unknown.

George Washington and Lady Liberty are sharing thoughts: "It's all very well, George, for you to keep your birthday in sight; but as you and I are twins, it's a little hard on me!"; Three young boys dressed as George Washington hold up the banner, "May you always enjoy a happy anniversary of Washington's Birthday." Artist signed HBG (HB Griggs). Published by L & E; Series No. 2242.

Abraham Lincoln

February 12, 1809 – April 15, 1865

Lincoln, the 16th President of the United States of America, has been ranked by scholars as being our country's second greatest President. He successfully preserved the Union by exercising great moral leadership by leading the country through a calamitous constitutional and military crisis: The American Civil War. Two episodic events promulgated by Lincoln forever placed him in the pantheon of great Americans: (1) The Emancipation Proclamation executive order issued on January 1, 1863, proclaiming the freedom of all slaves; and (2) His Gettysburg Address of November 1863, which is considered to be the most quoted political speech in U. S. history.

Abraham Lincoln's Log Cabin: Built by Abraham Lincoln and his father in 1831 in Coles' County, Illinois. Published by Abraham Lincoln Log Cabin Association.

Portrait of Abraham Lincoln. Copy of an original oil painted by Morris Katz.

Highlights of Lincoln's Life

• Lincoln was born in a one-room log cabin in Kentucky. As his family was experiencing some financial difficulties, they moved several times, eventually ending up in Illinois.

• In 1831, Lincoln struck out on his own, ending up in New Salem, Illinois, where he stayed for six years working at different types of jobs/trades as well as being a soldier in the Black Hawk War of 1832.

• During his years in New Salem, Lincoln started the study of law on his own and was admitted to the bar in 1836 while simultaneously winning several elections to the Illinois Assembly as a Whig in 1842.

• Lincoln became a successful prairie lawyer and, while studying under a mentor, he met and married Mary Todd in 1842. Over a period of years, during which time Lincoln moved his law office to Springfield, Illinois, he and his wife had four children; only two reached eighteen years of age.

Lincoln's portrait is highlighted at the bottom by the log cabin in which he was born at Rock Spring Farm, Kentucky, and at the top by the White House, where he lived as President. Published by International Art Publishing Co.; Series No. 51658.

An engraving by H. B. Hall of President Abraham Lincoln and Family. Mary Todd and their two sons, Thomas Lincoln and Robert Todd, are pictured in the background. A portrait of Washington hangs on the far wall.

Home of Abraham Lincoln in Springfield, Illinois. The home was purchased on May 2, 1844, and it was here that Lincoln lived when he was elected President. Photo by Larry Will. Published by Baxter Press.

• In 1846, Lincoln ran successfully for a two-year term in the Illinois House of Representatives as a Whig. Throughout his legal career, he continually spoke out against slavery, saying in part, "I hate it because it deprives our republican example of its just experience in the world."

• In 1858, the newly formed Republican Party nominated Lincoln for the U. S. Senate. His opponent was the Illinois Senior Senator Stephen A. Douglas. This campaign featured the seven Lincoln/Douglas debates, which are considered to be the most famous political debates in American history. The main issue was that of popular sovereignty and its expansion into U. S. free states. Lincoln lost this election, but gained much in terms of national political reputation.

In the background of Lincoln's portrait is his birthplace and also his home in Springfield, Illinois, where Lincoln lived with his family and worked as a lawyer.

- In 1860, the Illinois State Republican Party held its convention; Lincoln was nominated on the third ballot espousing moderation in slavery, protective tariffs, and modernization of the Government.
- On November 6, 1860, Abraham Lincoln was elected to be the 16th President of the United States. He was the first from the nascent Republican Party. Pre-slavery states had warned that if Lincoln was elected president they would secede from the Union and, on February 9, 1861, the Confederacy elected Jefferson Davis as their President.
- While Lincoln said that he did not want to interfere with slavery where it already existed, he also said that it was intolerable to dismantle the Union. The secessionists were equally strident in not wanting to rejoin the Union.
- In April 12, 1861, Southern troops fired upon Fort Sumter, South Carolina, initiating the opening shots of a war that would not see a conclusion until April 9, 1865, when Confederate General Robert E. Lee surrendered to General Ulysses S. Grant at Appomattox Court House, Virginia.
- During the mid-point of this bloody, fratricidal war, Lincoln issued his Emancipation Proclamation, giving freedom to over three million slaves (but not making them citizens) while promoting the passage of the 13th Amendment; this amendment, which finally abolished slavery, was ratified by the states by December 1865.
- On November 17, 1863, near the battlefield of Gettysburg, the scene of the bloodiest battle of the Civil War, Lincoln gave his two-minute Gettysburg Address. The speech brought to full fruition America's dedication to the principles of equal rights and liberty, and the survival of representative democracy whereby "the government of the people, by the people, for the people, shall not perish from the earth."

"Lincoln and the Contrabands": Lincoln is pictured with slaves, the idea of which he was against and became a main issue in the War Between the States. Published by Wolfe and Co. International Art Publishing Company.

This six-card set is known as the Lincoln Centennial Souvenir Series 1809-1909. Published by E. Nash; "Lincoln Birthday" Series No. 1.

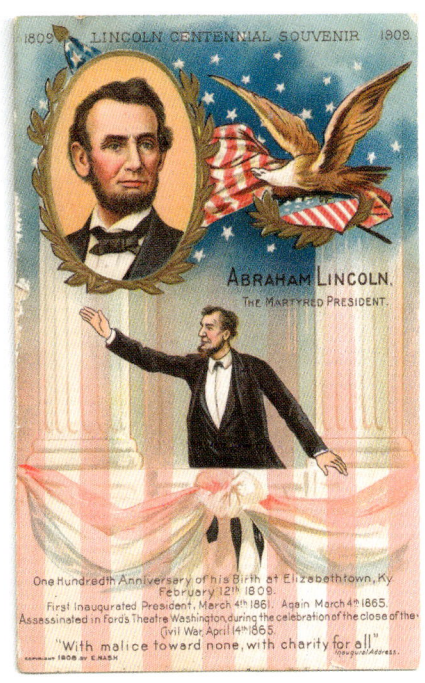

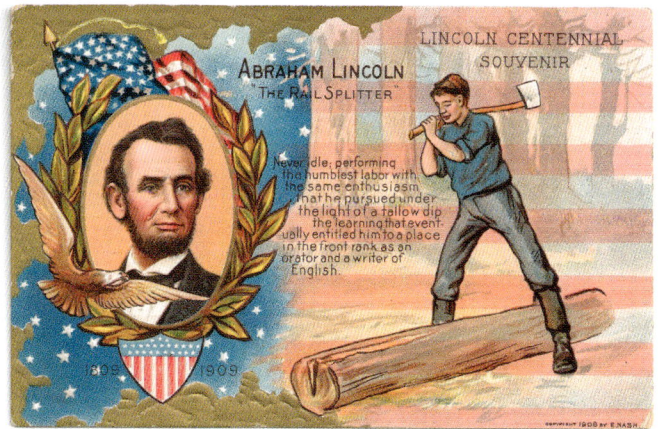

President Lincoln gives his Inaugural Address.

Abraham Lincoln, "the rail splitter": A young Lincoln is shown as enthusiastic and hard-working, which entitled him to "a place in the front rank as an orator and a writer of English."

President Lincoln is described as "A Man of Sorrow and Acquainted with Grief": A letter expressing this sorrow and grief was written by Lincoln to a Mother of five sons who have all died "gloriously on the battle field…as a sacrifice upon the altar of freedom."

"Lincoln's Emancipation Proclamation," was issued on January 1, 1863: "Henceforth a Government without a Master and without a Slave."

Lincoln is remembered as "immortalized by an oration on the occasion of the dedication of the National Cemetery at Gettysburg."

President Lincoln is pictured with two homes: Being born in the Log Cabin and now as President living in the White House.

- In the Presidential election of 1864, Lincoln was re-elected in a landslide. Now his job was to reunite the country, but not alienate the South through the mechanism of Reconstruction.
- Five days after the conclusion of the Civil War, on April 14, 1865, President Lincoln and his wife attended a play at Ford's Theatre. Confederate sympathizer John Wilkes Booth went to Lincoln's unguarded box and shot the President at point-blank range. The next morning Lincoln passed away.
- The assassin, Booth, was tracked down by Union soldiers and killed on April 24th on a farm in Virginia thirty miles south of Washington D. C.
- President Lincoln is interred in a family tomb at Oak Ridge Cemetery outside Springfield, Illinois. Mary Todd Lincoln and three of their four children are also entombed there.
- Lincoln's Birthday, while never having been selected as a Federal holiday, is a legal holiday in seven states and is observed on February 12th of each year.

"Inauguration of Abraham Lincoln." Published by Tuck & Sons; "Lincoln's Birthday" Series No. 155.

Statue of Lincoln and a slave honoring the Emancipation Proclamation with a flag and crown of laurel in the foreground. Published by Tuck & Sons; "Lincoln's Birthday" Series No. 155.

"Lincoln's Address at Gettysburg" is considered by many as one of the greatest political speeches of all times. Published by Tuck & Sons; "Lincoln's Birthday" Series No. 155.

"With malice towards none, with charity for all": President Lincoln's entry into Richmond, Virginia, on April 4, 1865. Published by International Art Publishing Co.; Series No. 51658.

Copy of a poster illustrating the assassination of President Lincoln by John Wilkes Booth at Ford's Theater. Artist is unknown.

Lady Liberty holds a crown of laurel to honor Lincoln. Artist signed C. Chapman. Published by International Art Publishing Co.; Series No. 51658.

Lincoln's statue (by Augustus Saint-Gaudens) overlooks the Capitol. Artist signed C. Chapman. Published by International Art Publishing Co.; Series No. 51658.

"Lincoln Centennial Grand March 1809-1909" song sheet. Composed by E. T. Paull (no words). Cover includes images of Lincoln's Birthplace, Lincoln's Memorial Hall, Emancipation Statue in Washington, and Lincoln's Tomb in Springfield, Illinois, that encompasses the portrait of Lincoln. Original. 1909.

Chapter 5

Memorial Day (Decoration Day)

Situated between Washington's Birthday and Independence Day, MEMORIAL DAY is a day set aside for sorrowful remembrance of our long-departed fighting men and women. In a perfect world, there would be no need for military cemeteries nor would we have to hear the mournful sounds of "Taps" as it spreads like a fog over the gravestones of the fallen.

Unfortunately, it is not a perfect world. Since the start of the American Revolutionary War in 1775 to present time, America has been involved in sixty-five engagements that have created battle casualties and/or wounded. In those 237 years, there have been 848,275 recorded deaths from combat and 495,650 deaths from non-combat, totaling 1,343,925 deaths from all conflicts. To visualize the enormity of total conflict deaths, these equal the population of San Antonio, Texas, the seventh largest city in the United States. The three greatest number of casualties occurred in the American Civil War with 625,000 deaths, followed by World War II with 405,400 deaths and World War I with 116,516 deaths. The casualties of the next three wars — Vietnam, Korea, and the American Revolutionary War — barely add up to the total casualties of the World War I conflict.

To commemorate our deceased veterans who have died either in war, deployment, or peacetime, burial plots are available through the Veterans Affairs Cemetery Administration, which maintains 131 national cemeteries in thirty-nine states and Puerto Rico. The Department of the Army maintains two national cemeteries — Arlington National Cemetery (250,000 gravesites) and Soldiers' & Airmen Home National Cemetery. The Department of the Interior through the National Park Service maintains another fourteen national cemeteries. The American Battle Monuments Commission Cemeteries (ABMC), established in 1923 by Congress in order to commemorate the service, achievements, and sacrifice of the United States Armed Forces that have served overseas since 1917, maintains twenty-four cemeteries overseas for 125,000 American war dead and monuments for another 94,000 U. S. servicemen and women who are either unidentified or missing in action.

Memorial Day, a Federal holiday celebrated on the last Monday in May, was originally known as DECORATION DAY. The first "unofficial" documented tribute to the American Civil War dead occurred in Columbus, Mississippi, on April 25, 1866 (one year after the war's end), when local women visited a cemetery to decorate the graves of Confederate soldiers killed at the Battle of Shiloh. The women noticed that graves located nearby of fallen Union soldiers were unattended and bare, so the good ladies also decorated them. In the years directly after the Civil War, there were many other localized commemorations both in the North and the South.

On May 5, 1868 (three years after the Civil War ended), Major General John A. Logan, the head of a large organization of Union veterans — the Grand Army of the Republic (GAR) — established Decoration Day as a time for the nation to decorate the graves of the war dead with flowers and other festive ribbons. General Logan declared that Decoration Day be observed on May 30th of any given year. In this first Decoration Day, General Logan gave an order to decorate the graves "with the choicest flowers of springtime" while urging that "we should guard their graves with sacred vigilance." The first large observance of Decoration Day, held in that same year at Arlington National Cemetery, was attended by 5,000 visitors. Some of the very first interred at Arlington in 1864 were 1,800 Union dead from the First Battle of Bull Run.

In the Deep South, besides the many localized memorial events, there are nine "official" state holiday observances to honor those who died fighting for the Confederate States of America. Confederate Memorial Day is observed in Alabama, Florida, Georgia, Louisiana, Mississippi, North Carolina, and South Carolina usually on selected dates in late April or early May. Tennessee celebrates Confederate Decoration Day on June 3rd, which is the birth date of Jefferson Davis, the first and only President of the Confederacy. Texas observes two memorial days: Confederate Heroes Day on January 19th, which is the state's "official" holiday (combining

The first card honors U. S. Grant and R. E. Lee while the second card honors the U.S.A. and the C.S.A. Flags and laurel leaves decorate both cards. Published by Winsch.

the previously official state holidays of Robert E. Lee and Jefferson Davis), and Confederate Memorial Day on April 26th, where many organizations and communities observe a separate commemorative day.

Many communities both north and south of the Mason-Dixon line have laid claim to being the birthplace of Memorial Day: fourteen from the South and ten from the north. However, in May 1966 President Lyndon B. Johnson, on the behalf of the U. S. Government, sanctioned Waterloo, New York, as the "official" birthplace of Memorial Day because of the town's 100-year commitment to commemoration ceremonies that began on May 5, 1866.

In the late 1800s, the name Decoration Day started to be phased out in place of Memorial Day. In 1882, the Grand Old Army organization urged their members that the "proper designation of May 30th is Memorial Day — not Decoration Day." However, Decoration Day retained its identity well into the mid-twentieth century.

Many postcards of the early twentieth century bear the designation "Decoration Day" while others used the more encompassing "Memorial Day."

In 1967, the Federal Government officially changed the name of the Decoration Day observation to Memorial Day and, on June 28, 1968, Congress passed the Uniform Holidays Bill, which moved four holidays, including Memorial Day, from their traditional dates to a specific Monday in order to create a convenient three-day weekend. Eventually all fifty states adopted Congress's change of dates within a few years. Today Memorial Day is traditionally observed by patriotically tending to the graves at any number of national and state military cemeteries. For those servicemen and women who have given their lives for their country in war as well as peacetime, a national moment of remembrance takes place at 3 p.m. local time.

In these very collectible postcards, a Grandmother recalls the events of the Civil War while a young girl and boy visit the grave of the fallen soldier. "Strew the fair garlands where slumber the dead." Attributed to artist Frances Brundage. Published by Tuck & Sons; "Decoration Day Series" No. 173, a set of twelve cards published in 1910.

Series No. 973 honors the Grand Army of the Republic Veteran, whose initials (GAR) are highlighted on the cards, and urges people to remember the soldiers' grand sacrifice: "Lest we forget" shows soldiers marching in a wreath of flowers and "Nor shall their story be forgot" shows innocent children with the flag and a wreath of flowers. Artist signed Ellen Clapsaddle. Published by International Art Publishing Company.

Series No. 150 is a set of ten unsigned cards by artist Frances Brundage, one of the country's busiest and most successful commercial artist of her era. In addition to postcards, she illustrated children's storybooks, including such classics as *Pinocchio* and *Robinson Crusoe*, and paper toys and dolls. This series is considered one of the most beautiful collections of Decoration Day postcards. Published by San Gabriel Company.

Three cards honoring the fallen soldiers. "GAR" in highly decorative scroll is the central image on two of the cards with colorful flower petals in the background. In true Clapsaddle form, the first card shows an innocent-faced child in his Civil War uniform holding a flag honoring the fallen soldier: "On Fame's eternal camping ground their silent tents are spread." Artist signed Ellen Clapsaddle. Published by International Art Publishing Company; Series No. 2444.

Children, one in his Union Army uniform and the other dressed as a Navy Seaman, with pink and white flowers wave flags to honor the dead. Slogans – "Lest we forget," "Nor shall their story be forgot," and "the Army and Navy forever!" – decorate the cards. Artist signed Ellen Clapsaddle. Published by International Art Publishing Company.

Bordered by blue this outstanding series features Grant and Lee shaking hands ("Under One Flag"), a woman mourning at the grave of a fallen soldier ("They Gave Their All"), a couple hidden by the flag ("Story of the Flag"), and a young girl and boy dressed in blue and gray ("The Blue and The Gray"). Both the South and the North are honored in these postcards. Artist signed C. Bunnell. Published by Fred Lounsbury; Series 2083.

The young and the old honor the fallen soldiers with flags and wreaths. A Union veteran now greets a present-day soldier; an older woman decorates the portrait of a Union veteran; a young lady decorates a grave with garlands as Lady Liberty honors two soldiers shaking hands; and an older gentleman ponders the past. Published by Tuck & Sons; "Decoration Day" Series No. 158, a set of twelve cards published in 1909.

A very unique postcard – it is part of an unnumbered set of twelve published by Tuck & Sons that was sold almost exclusively in the South in 1908. These postcards were scarce and almost impossible for a collector to amass. The Confederate set pictures southern flags, as well as the South's leaders and generals. Unlike Tuck's cards for the North, which were called "Decoration Day," this set is titled "Memorial Day."

145

"Soldier, rest! Thy warfare o'er, Sleep the sleep that know not-breaking." A Civil War Veteran takes his hat off to commemorate both Union and Confederate soldiers and lays roses at the grave of a fellow soldier. Published by Tuck & Sons.

"The desolate Mourners go, lovingly laden with flowers. Alike for the friend and the foe: Under the sod and the dew, waiting the judgment day, under the roses The Blue, under the lilies The Gray." Published by Nash; "Decoration Day" Series No. 1.

American flags and a special banner featuring Lady Liberty crowning all Civil War soldiers with a laurel wreath are held high as marching soldiers show their respect. Published by Tuck & Sons; Series No. 107, a set of twelve cards published in 1908.

A granddaughter pins a red rose on her grandfather proudly dressed in his Union blues; a grandson dressed in his Civil War uniform together with hat, badge, and sword recalls his Grandfather's memories; the badge of the Grand Army of the Republic, along with medals of the war years and a wreath of roses, honors the fallen soldiers; a young girl takes bouquets of red roses to be laid upon the tombs on the fallen heroes. Published by Winsch; "Decoration Day" Series No. 3.

A veteran Union soldier linked arm-in-arm with a United States soldier "Today and Yesterday"; a young nurse as a member of the Womans Relief Corps holds the flag of the American Red Cross; a young Daughter of the Regiment holds a flag as a wreath of red roses drapes her arm; a U.S. soldier is surrounded by a laurel wreath as he honors "To my Comrade." Published by Nash; "Decoration Day" Series No. 2.

A Union soldier lays a wreath of roses and ties a bow on the American flag as he honors a fellow veteran; a Union soldier and a Confederate soldier having lost an arm in the war shake hands at the gravesite of a fallen comrade. Both postcards are bordered by red and white flags and gold stars. Published by Nash; "Decoration Day" Series No. 4.

"Memorial Day" – This patriotic postcard patriotic features the Capitol, a Union soldier beating a drum with the Pledge of Allegiance written on it, the flag, and laurel wreaths, which are a symbol of victory. Published by Winsch.

The Bald Eagle and the American Flag drape the grave and the cannon; cannonballs with wreaths of roses and laurel branches lay in the foreground. Published by Santway; Series No. 157.

Memorial Day – "Loyalty has reunited the country. Where the cannon once stood, now stands the Angel of Peace reuniting the North and the South. One People. One Flag. One Country." Published by Winsch.

148

"Honor the Brave 1861-1865." Various scenes as the community honors soldiers at the cemetery; placing flags on graves and listening to speeches commemorating the lives of the fallen. Artist signed W. F. Burger. Publisher is unknown; Series 625.

Memorial Day is celebrated with three different scenes: A couple reverently raises the flag; a mother and her children dressed in their finery take lilies, representing the southern states, and roses, representing the northern states, to honor the fallen soldiers; and Lady Liberty, holding a bouquet of roses, casts them on the gravestone. Artist C. Chapman. Published by International Art Publishing Company.

The Red, White, and Blue take center stage on these three postcards with Memorial Day Greetings. Publisher is unknown; Series 815.

Three postcards glorify three patriots: Lincoln's Monument, Springfield, Illinois – In Memoriam to those who died for us; General Grant's Tomb, New York City – In Memoriam to those who fought for us; Washington's Tomb, Mt. Vernon, Virginia – In Memoriam to our dead patriots. Published by Winsch; "Decoration Series" No. 5.

Fallen soldiers are honored with "Peace" and "Honor the Brave" as the central themes on these four cards. Angels dressed in pink carry garlands of laurel leaves to honor the dead from West, North, East, and South. Cannons, cannonballs, and guns are surrounded by flags. Published by M. W. Taggart; Series 603 and 604.

Two Memorial Day souvenir postcards: One shows a flag proudly flying over a cannon while the second features a gravestone decorated with flowers. Published by Santway; Series 157.

Bordered with gold and sparkling silver, these five postcards depict the soldier's life: "As we are marching through Georgia," in their tent camps, on guard along the Potomac, and honoring a fallen soldier. Flowers decorate one of the cards, "Their's is a deathless heritage: their deeds blossom like flowers upon the field of time. And whether told in prose or glowing rhyme, seem writ in shining gold to him who reads." Published by Winsch.

Chapter 6

Veterans Day (Armistice Day)

VETERANS DAY is a Federal holiday that honors all living veterans of the United States Armed Forces, whether or not they have served in a conflict. This holiday is often confused with Memorial Day, which honors the deceased veterans of the United States Armed Forces. For example, Frank Buckles, who was a member of the U. S. Army was the oldest remaining World War I veteran alive until he passed away on February 27, 2011, at the age of 110 years. As a veteran, his country honored him, and as a deceased veteran, his country gratefully remembers him.

Veterans Day is strictly observed on November 11th of each year; therefore this holiday is not part of the Uniform Monday Holiday Act that gives workers a three-day weekend. November 11th is a celebrated important date worldwide because it marks the exact time the major hostilities of World War I in Europe were officially ended: the 11th hour, of the 11th day, of the 11th month of 1918. That gave rise to the recognition that it was "All Quiet on the Western Front." The other major powers in this conflict also observe November 11th; in some United Kingdom countries, it is known as Remembrance Day.

The European War ended with the 11-11-11 armistice signed among combatants in a railroad car in France. However, a formal declaration was needed to effectively conclude the war as well as extract reparations from the Central Powers (Germany, Austria, and Hungary). Therefore, the Paris Peace Conference began on January 12, 1919, as the delegates from twenty-seven Allied Countries began to discuss and set forth a laundry list of treaty demands on the Central Powers. Nearly six months later the treaty demands were "accepted" by Germany and the Treaty of Versailles (Treaty of Peace) was signed on June 28, 1919, which formally concluded the "Great War" to end all wars.

Interestingly enough, the United States was NOT a signatory to the Treaty. The Treaty set up the League of Nations (much like today's United Nations), but to become a member there was a Covenant — Article X maintained that a member country would be bound by international contract to defend another League of Nation member from attack. The Republican isolationists in Woodrow Wilson's Administration defeated all efforts for America to join due to that Covenant. Eventually, during Warren G. Harding's Administration, a joint resolution was passed and a separate treaty ending the United States' involvement in World War I was signed on July 21, 1921, without America having to become a member of the League of Nations.

The Flag Bearer stands in front of a V-shaped group of servicemen and women, each wearing a historic uniform from the past.

Veterans Day, November 11, 2001. Limited Edition Disney Pin, 1-1/2" tall.

Council of Four at the Versailles Peace Conference: L-R: Lloyd George, Vittorio Emanuele Orlando, Georges Clemenceau, and President Woodrow Wilson. U. S. Signal Corps photo by Edward Jackson, May 27, 1919.

The Treaty of Versailles was signed on June 28, 1919, after which President Woodrow Wilson wanted to focus the citizenry on the sacrifices of America's involvement in World War I in terms of manpower. Therefore, Wilson issued a proclamation declaring that November 11, 1919, should be known as Armistice Day. His proclamation in part said:

To us in America, the reflections of Armistice Day will be filled with solemn pride in the heroism of those who died in the country's service and with gratitude for the victory, both because of the thing from which it has freed us and because of the opportunity it has given America to show her sympathy with peace and justice in the councils of the nations.

On the actual Armistice Day in 1918 there were wild celebrations in each of the major cities in the United States. From the time of President Wilson's proclamation, Armistice Day has been celebrated annually in America; its name was changed to Veterans Day in 1954.

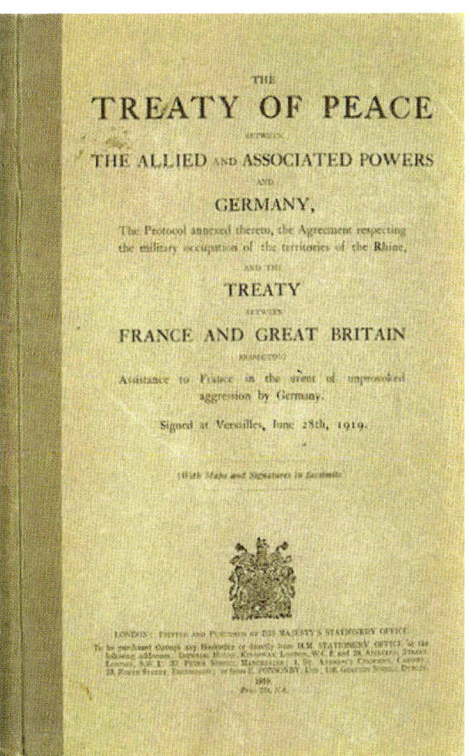

"Joy in New York at News of Signing of Armistice." Original Rotogravure: Photograph shows scene of "Delighted Populace at Fifth Avenue and Fortieth Street, New York City…" *New York Times*, November 11, 1918. 10 1/2" x 13"

Document: The Treaty of Peace, a publication in English signed at Versailles, France, June 28, 1919 formally ending hostilities between Germany and the Triple Entente (Allied Powers). Original located in Versailles, France.

*Scenes from Arlington Cemetery, 2011.
Photographer unknown.*

A Wreath at the Tomb of the Unknown Soldier, Arlington Cemetery, Washington D. C.

Joint Colors Post in Advance of the President, Arlington Cemetery.

National Veterans Day Observance, Memorial Amphitheater, Arlington Cemetery.

In order to have a permanent place of honor for those service members who died in combat but whose remains were never identified, Congress, on March 4, 1921, approved the burial of an identified American serviceman from World War I in the Plaza of the new memorial Amphitheater in Arlington Cemetery. Therefore, the Tomb of the Unknown Soldier was established, made from American marble and constructed as a three-level tomb. A chosen casket of remains was brought from France and the World War I Unknown lay in state in the Capitol Rotunda until Armistice Day 1921. On November 11th, President Warren G. Harding officiated at the interment ceremonies at Arlington Cemetery. In 1932, a new four-level tomb was placed in the same location. The Western panel of the tomb is inscribed with the following words:

HERE RESTS IN
HONORED GLORY
AN AMERICAN SOLDIER
KNOWN BUT TO GOD

Since then two more Unknown Soldier crypts from World War II and Korea have been established. A Vietnam War crypt was also placed, but now remains empty as the interred remains were positively identified by DNA tests. With these additional crypts in place, the area is now called the Tomb of the Unknowns. The Veterans Day National Ceremony is held each year on November 11th at Arlington Cemetery. The ceremony commences precisely at 11 a.m. with a formal wreath-laying at the Tomb of the Unknowns by the President of the United States. A bugler sounds "Taps," and the ceremony continues inside the Memorial Amphitheater with a Parade of Flags by veterans' organizations and remarks from invited dignitaries.

Christmas Wreaths at Arlington National Cemetery. More than 5,000 donated Christmas wreaths were laid against headstones in December 2005. *Arlington National Cemetery Photograph.*

The Tomb of the Unknown Soldier-Tomb Guards

Probably the most elite Honor Guard in the world is the Unknown Soldier Tomb Guards called Sentinels. While there are many falsehoods concerning these Sentinels, a few proven facts are in order.

• The Tomb Guards (men and women) work on a three Relief (team) rotation — 24 hours on, 24 hours off, 24 hours on, 24 hours off, 24 hours on, 96 hours off. Their tour of duty last approximately one year.

• The Guard is changed every thirty minutes during the summer (April 1 to September 30) and every hour during the winter (October 1 to March 31) when Arlington Cemetery is open. During the hours the cemetery is closed, the Guard is changed every two hours. The Tomb is guarded twenty-four hours a day, seven days a week, and every minute of the day since July 2, 1937, regardless of most weather conditions.

• During the Guard's walk across the Tomb of the Unknowns, the Guard takes twenty-one steps, which conforms to the twenty-one gun salute, the highest honor given to any military or foreign dignitary. The Guard, after completing his/her twenty-one steps, turns and faces the Tomb for twenty-one seconds. Then the Guard turns to face back down the mat, changes his/her weapon to the outside shoulder, counts twenty-one seconds,

Guard at the Tomb of the Unknowns in Arlington National Cemetery. *Arlington National Cemetery Photograph.*

and then steps off for another twenty-one step walk down the mat. The Guard then faces the Tomb at each end of the twenty-one step walk for twenty-one seconds done repeatedly until relieved at the Guard Change.

This is the highest honor that a member of the United States Army can ascribe. "Many apply but few are chosen."

On June 4, 1926, Congress passed a resolution that the "recurring anniversary of November 11, 1918, should be commemorated with thanksgiving and prayer…" By that time twenty-seven states had made November 11th a state holiday. On May 13, 1938, an Act of Congress made November 11th a legal Federal holiday, but this holiday was still called Armistice Day. After World War II and the Korean War, various veterans' organizations lobbied Congress to amend the 1938 Act, striking the word Armistice in favor of Veterans Day. President Dwight D. Eisenhower signed this amendment on June 1, 1954, establishing Veterans Day on November 11th as a day to honor all American veterans — living or dead — of all wars but especially living veterans who have served their country honorably during war or peace.

There are 23.4 million veterans alive today who warrant our respect. There are parades to commemorate Veterans Day and other community festivities, such as patriotic band concerts. It is also proper for citizens to observe a few moments of silence at the appropriate hour of 11 a.m. local time.

Finally, and very important, is the fact that over ten percent of veterans alive today are disabled from service-related disabilities. With the survival rate of recuperation from horrific battlefield injuries increasing due to excellent field hospital care, there are many disabled veterans from continuing conflicts that need our help. Unfortunately, wounded veterans from conflicts occurring in the nineteenth and twentieth centuries were, in many cases, left to fend for themselves; many who did not have family support went homeless and, in many cases, died where they lain… and perhaps "unknown."

Bookmark decorated with red poppies – "Veterans Day. The armistice that ended 'The Great War' World War I was signed on the 11th hour of the 11th day of the 11th month. November 11th, 1918, Armistice Day Remembrance Day."

Veterans Day Parade, Oakland, California, November, 1954. Photographer unknown.

Sons of Veterans: "A fame that clusters bright around the brows of leaders laurel crowned and honored heroes neath the ground." Remembrance of the Veterans of the American Civil War. Embossed. Publisher is unknown; "Decoration Day" Series No.1.

"Armistice Day Forever" sheet music. Written by Berry J. Sisk. Introduced by Sousa's Band. Adopted as the Official March of the American Legion. Original. 1922.

"It was a touching scene." A threadbare veteran wears his sign: "I lost my legs" pushing himself in a little red wagon while holding out his hat in hopes for help from someone in his homeland represented by the red, white, and blue wearing "patriot." This scene was all too frequent in the aftermath of World War I and World War II. Publisher is unknown.

Red Poppies

The Veterans of Foreign Wars conducted its first paper poppy distribution before Decoration Day in 1922. The red poppy, evocative of the red poppies that grew on French and Belgium battlefields, was soon adopted as the official memorial flower of the VFW. It was during the 1923 encampment of this veterans organization that it decided that Buddy Poppies would be assembled by disabled veterans who would then be paid for their work to provide them with some form of financial assistance. In February 1924, the VFW registered the name "Buddy Poppy" with the U. S. Patent Office. This trademark guarantees that all poppies bearing that name and the VFW label are genuine artificial products made by disabled veterans. Today, VFW Buddy Poppies are still assembled by disabled veterans at Veterans Administration Hospitals. The funds from the sale of these poppies also partially support the VFW/National Home for orphans and widows of our nation's veterans. The red poppy is also a key symbol for Remembrance Day in Great Britain.

One of the most beloved and poignant war memorial poems that evolved from World War I brought to light the symbiosis between life and death. The author, Canadian Lt. Col. John McCrae, wrote the poem on May 3, 1915, after the burial of a friend who was killed in action. Lt. Col. McCrae also did not survive the Great War; he died January 28, 1918.

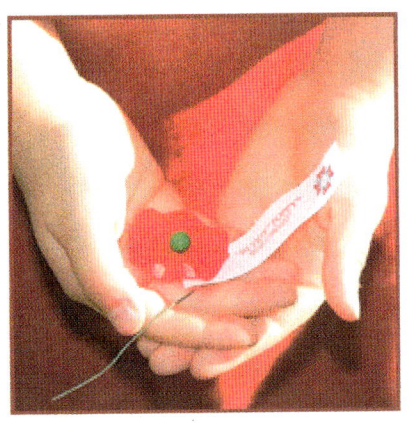

Buddy Poppy: Two examples of handmade poppies. Buddy Poppy proceeds provide no profit to any VFW unit. Instead all public contributions are used in the cause of veterans or for the wellbeing of their dependents. *Images from advertisement flier distributed by the VFW.*

In Flanders Fields the poppies blow
Between the crosses, row on row
That mark our place; and in the sky
The larks, still bravely singing fly
Scarce heard amid the guns below.
We are the dead. Short days ago
We lived, felt dawn, saw sunset glow
Loved and were loved and now we lie
In Flanders Fields.
Take up our quarrel with the foe:
To you, from failing hands, we throw
The torch, be yours to hold it high.
If ye break faith with us, who die
We shall not sleep, though the poppies grow
  In Flanders Fields.

"Filii Veteranorum" Sons of Veterans are honored by this embossed card. Publisher is unknown; "Decoration Day" Series No. 2.

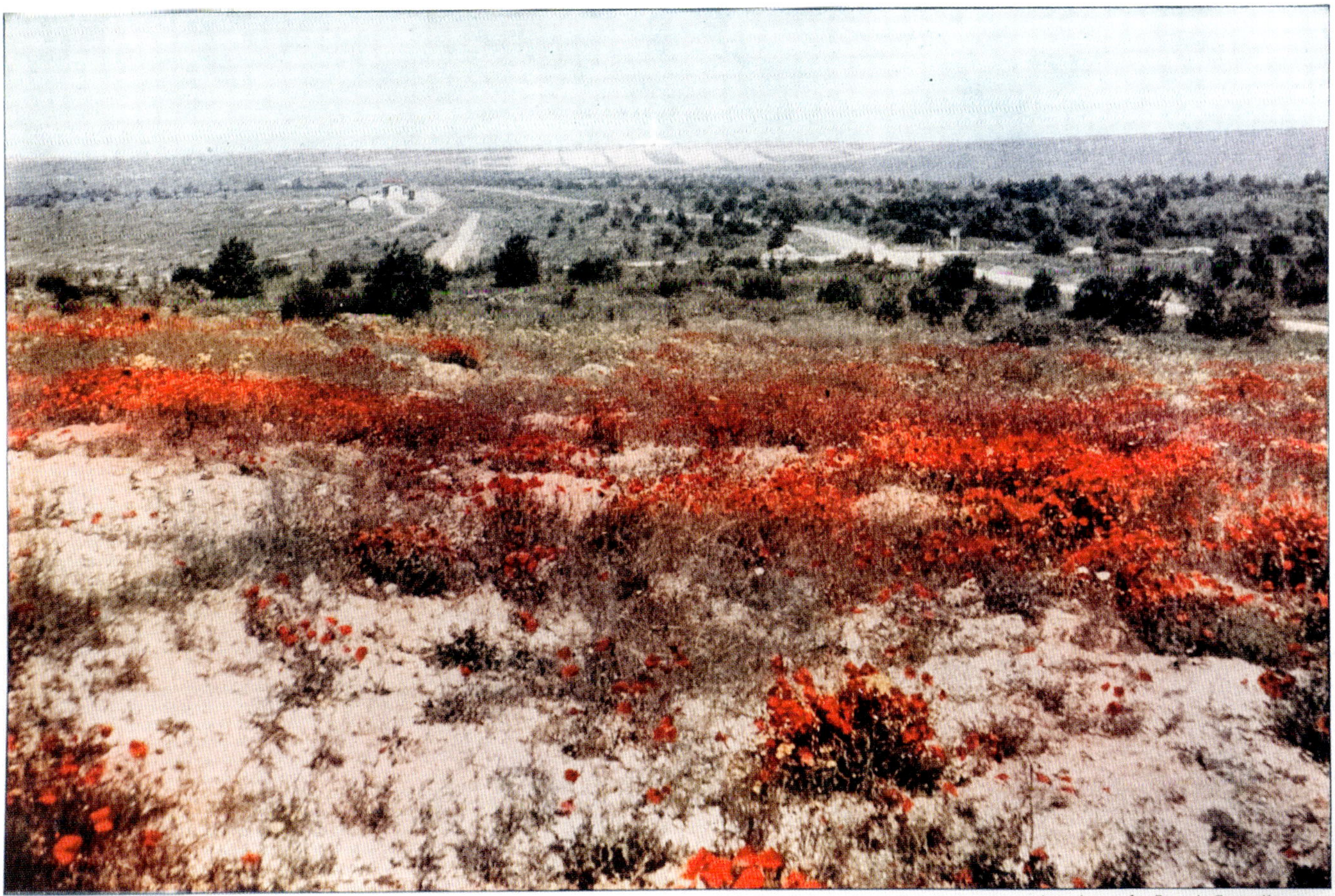
© National Geographic Society
Autochrome by Gervais Courtellemont
THE FIELD OF VERDUN EVER WILL REMAIN A MONUMENT TO THE VALOR OF FRANCE

Poppy fields tend to bloom on battlefields whether it be Flanders Field or Verdun, France. Photographed by Gervais Courtellemont, *National Geographic*, 1929.

11/11/1918
Today

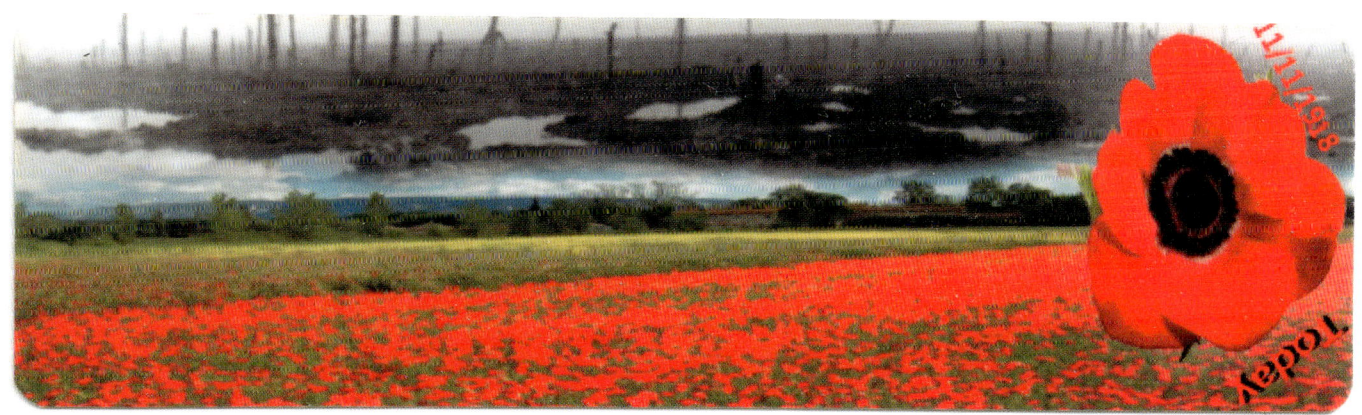

Bookmark showing Flanders Fields at the end of the war as a devastated landscape and today in full bloom with vivid red poppies.

Chapter 7

Columbus Day

COLUMBUS DAY is the only Federal holiday in the United States that is physically celebrated in other parts of the world. In Spain, in many countries in Latin and South America, and even in the Bahamas, the anniversary of Christopher Columbus's arrival in the Americas, which occurred October 12, 1492, is celebrated as an official holiday.

As the case with many of America's Federal holidays, the celebration of Columbus Day first started out as local city events, followed by state holidays, before eventually becoming one of eleven Federal holidays. The first reported Columbus Day observance in the United States occurred in New York City in 1792, where the Tercentennial (300th) anniversary of Columbus's voyage to the New World was celebrated. In 1892, during President Benjamin Harrison's Administration, he called upon the citizens of the United States to observe Columbus Day on its Quadricentennial (400th) anniversary, which was used to personify America's increasingly anti-isolationist stance on its way to becoming a world leader. However, there were certainly more "discoveries" to be made in world affairs.

Since Christopher Columbus was of Italian (Genoese) ethnicity, Italian-Americans in the United States observed Columbus Day as a celebration of their heritage much like Irish-Americans celebrate St. Patrick's Day. As an ample amount of immigrants to America in the late nineteenth century were Italian Roman Catholics, and many centered in the large eastern seaboard cities, it seemed fitting that the first post-war celebration of Columbus Day was held in New York City on October 12, 1866. Two years later, in 1868, an Italian-American in San Francisco founded the oldest continuously existing celebration with a Columbus Day parade. In 2011, San Francisco's 143rd Annual Italian Heritage Parade was held as the city's oldest civic event as well as the nation's oldest Italian-American parade honoring Columbus.

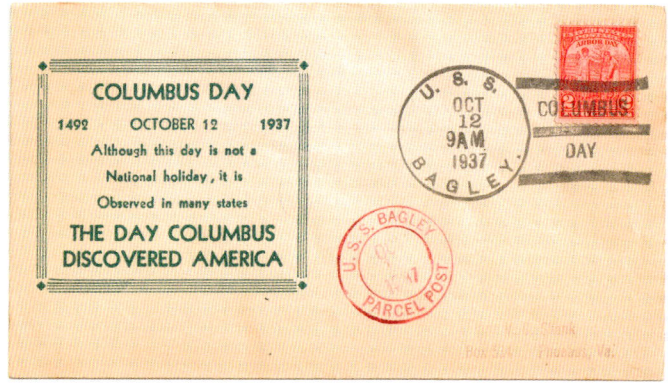

Ship Cancellation: *USS Bagley*, dated October 12, 1937. Cover has printed Columbus Day cachet. Many United States naval vessels of the 1930s used holiday cachets on envelopes as a means to enhance communications between the sender and the recipients.

A visage of Christopher Columbus along with his three ships. First day cover dated October 12, 1932, Columbus, Wisconsin.

However, it took an Irish-American Catholic priest, The Venerable Father Michael J. McGivney, to establish the Knights of Columbus on March 29, 1882. Since Catholics of all ethnicity were generally excluded from joining labor unions and fraternal organizations that provided social services, Father McGivney founded the Knights Order to be a mutual benefit society. The name "Columbus" was chosen for two reasons: (1) To send a message to the Protestant leadership in the country who honored Columbus as a hero that it was, in fact, a Catholic that was a contributory factor in the founding of the Americas; and (2) Because within ten years the 400th Anniversary of Columbus's arrival in the New World would be again observed and it would be a time of renewed interest in him. This was true because the World Columbian Exposition was held in Chicago, Illinois, in 1893, and visited by more than 27 million people over a six-month period.

As a result of a lobbying effort by the Knights of Columbus in 1906, the U. S. Congress approved, in 1907, the appropriation of $100,000 for the design and construction of a memorial fountain. On June 8, 1912, at the Union Station Plaza in Washington D.C., the Christopher Columbus Memorial Fountain was dedicated with a parade featuring more than 80,000 participants in front of an estimated crowd of 150,000. The Columbus Fountain, made of marble, is a semi-circular double-basin fountain with a shaft forty-five feet tall. The front of the shaft bears a full-length, fifteen feet high sculpture of Christopher Columbus. Designed by Loredo Taft, the fountain also contains other symbolic sculptures, such as a Native American facing West representing the "New World" and a bearded elderly man facing East representing the "Old World" flanked by eagles. At this fountain, Columbus Day is observed annually with a wreath-laying ceremony accompanied by the U. S. Marine Corps Band. In 2012, the 100th anniversary of the dedication of this fountain will be held.

While the New York and San Francisco parades were local events, another Italian-American, Angelo Noce, was able to get the Colorado Governor to declare the first official Columbus Day holiday for the state in 1905. Other states soon followed. By 1934, as a result of lobbying by the Knights of Columbus, President Franklin Delano Roosevelt and Congress set aside October 12th, Columbus Day, as a Federal holiday. However, several states do not recognize Columbus Day as a holiday because either the date, October 12th, falls close to another state holiday or as a form of protest against the alleged treatment of Native Americans by the Spanish who came with or after Columbus and his many voyages.

View toward The Administration Building overlooking the Canal of Venice for the World Columbian Exposition in 1893. Painting by Thomas Moran (1837-1926). Original located in the Brooklyn Museum in Brooklyn, New York.

The Christopher Columbus Memorial, Union Station Plaza, Washington, D.C. Postcard published by I. & M. Ottenheimer, Baltimore, Maryland.

One of the legacies from the voyages of Christopher Columbus was that the name Columbia was first used in lieu of America by the British Parliament in 1738. In the last two decades of the eighteenth century, the name Columbia became the name of the country's capital as the District of Columbia. As reviewed earlier in this book, the iconic personification of America as the female Columbia spread quickly and was in great use as a domestic version of Uncle Sam well into the twentieth century. Due to the apogee of Columbus's popularity coinciding with the World Columbian Exposition in 1893, numerous cities and towns were either renamed or named after him including the capital cities of two states, Ohio and South Carolina.

Columbia wearing a laurel wreath while carrying the American flag as well as red, white, and blue flowers. A most impressive card. Publisher is unknown.

Envelopes: Set of sixteen covers with six different engraved cachets depicting a scene from Christopher Columbus' first voyage to the New World, dated October 12, 1932, and addressed to the same recipient. Each envelope is individually cancelled with each state that has a city, town, or village named "Columbus." The states shown here are as follows (L to R, Top to Bottom): Mississippi, Montana, North Dakota, Kansas, Ohio, New York, Michigan, New Jersey, Georgia, Illinois, New Mexico, Wisconsin, Indiana, Kentucky, Nebraska, and Texas. Today there are thirty towns in the United States named "Columbus."

Christopher Columbus

Columbus was born in Genoa (Republic of Genoa), now in present-day Italy, in the time between August and October, 1451. He died at the age of fifty-four on May 20, 1506, in Valladolid, Crown of Castile, now in present-day Spain. He led an exciting life as a combination maritime explorer, navigator, and New World colonizer. After accumulating twelve valuable years of sailing experience, Columbus approached King John II of Portugal in 1485 and 1488 for three ships, men, and capital to navigate a passage westward across the "Ocean Sea" to the "Indies." He was turned down twice by King John due to: (1) Columbus's estimate of the distance westerly was far too small; and (2) Another explorer showed that a potential eastern sea route to Asia was now feasible. Undaunted, Columbus approached the Catholic monarchs, Ferdinand II of Aragon and Queen Isabella I of Castile, in 1486 (while waiting for King John to give his answer) to judge any interest in his venture. Six more years passed until, in 1492, Columbus finally persevered in his quest and received a positive response from the monarchs.

With financial backing from Ferdinand and Isabella, the Italian-born explorer was intent on charting a western sea route to China, India, and Japan, as well as to the mysterious gold and spice islands of Asia. If he succeeded, Columbus was to be given the title of "Admiral of the Ocean Sea" and would be appointed Viceroy and Governor of all the new lands he could claim for Spain as well as a portion of the profits.

In summary, Christopher Columbus completed four round-trip voyages between the years of 1492 and 1503, all of which were sponsored financially by the Castilian monarchs. The cost/benefit ratio of these voyages was tremendously profitable, not particularly in terms of valuables but in terms of being the genesis of European exploration and the eventual profitable colonization of the American continent. While the Norseman Leif Ericson was reputedly the very first explorer to set foot on North American land, at the northern tip of Newfoundland, called Vinland, around A.D. 1000, he left no permanent settlement, so Columbus had the honor of being the first explorer to initiate the same nearly five hundred years later.

Photo reproduction of a Posthumous portrait of Christopher Columbus by Sebastiano del Piombo. There are no known authentic drawn or painted likenesses of Columbus. Original painting, 1519, located at the Metropolitan Museum of Art.

First Voyage: August 3, 1492-March 15, 1493

Columbus departed from Palos de la Frontera, Spain, with three ships: *Santa Maria*, a carrack type ship one hundred feet in length; and the *Pinta* and *Nina*, both caravel ships approximately fifty feet long. There were ninety crew members among the three boats. In one month's time, they reached the Canary Islands for supplies and repairs. Three days later, on September 6, 1492, the ships departed the Canaries for what turned out to be a five-week voyage across the Atlantic Ocean. They reached landfall on October 12, 1492. Columbus named the small island San Salvador while the natives on the island called it Guanahani. This area, with its surrounding islands, is now called the Bahamas. Before leaving, Columbus established Spain's first colony in the Americas on the northern island of Hispaniola, named La Navidad, with thirty-nine of his men. When Columbus returned on his second voyage, nothing remained of the fortress or his men.

There exists, to this day, controversy as to which exact island Columbus made his initial landfall. There are about ten possibilities, each with their advocates. However, over the past five years, this field has been narrowed down to two. From its own research, the *National Geographic* selected Samana Cay as their choice of landfall. The author of *Columbus* has selected Watlings Island as his first landfall choice while researcher Keith A. Pickering has selected Plana Cays as the most logical landfall due to the science of magnetic declination whereby he recomputed a new westerly magnetic track given the speed of the *Santa Maria* for each hour of the voyage to arrive at a computer end of track. Plana Cays lies approximately forty miles SSE of Samana Cay. Columbus named the discovery island "San Salvador."

The next four islands he visited and named before reaching Juana (Cuba) were Santa Maria, Fernandina, Isabela, and Las Islas de Arena. After taking leave of Cuba, he proceeded in an easterly direction and skirted the northern coast of Espanola (Hispaniola—now Haiti and the Dominican Republic) before sailing back to Spain via the Azores Islands. During the trip home, the *Santa Maria* was wrecked so Columbus finished the voyage on the *Nina*.

Upon his arrival back to Spain at the court of Ferdinand and Isabella, he presented the monarchs with six or seven "indios" (he thought that he reached India so he called the captured natives indios), parrots, and other valuables.

The three ships — *Santa Maria*, *Pinta*, and *Nina* — that Columbus and his sailors used to sail to the New World. Publisher: Fritz Homann AG from Geschichte unserer Welt (*History of the World* pictures), late 1940s.

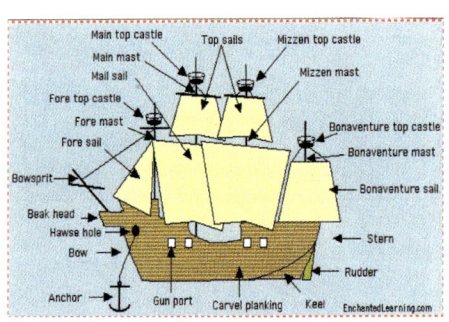

Schematic of the *Santa Maria*, a carrack (a three- or four-masted sailing vessel), showing sails location and configuration. This ship was approximately 30 to 36 meters long (98' to 118') and had a crew of approximately fifty seamen of varying duties. Image from Enchanted Learning, producer of children's learning activities.

Fanciful illustration of an island native welcoming the three ships of Columbus. Postcard publisher is unknown.

Antique Color Bookplates from the book *Columbus and Columbia*, published in 1893 by the Historical Publishing Company, Philadelphia, to celebrate the "Great Columbian Exposition" held in Chicago, Illinois. Plate No. 1: The First View of the New World; Plate No. 2: Columbus Taking Possession of the New World. Plate No. 3: Columbus' Return from the New World (and his arrival at the Court of Castile). *From the book Columbus and Columbia, published in 1893 by the Historical Publishing Company, Philadelphia.*

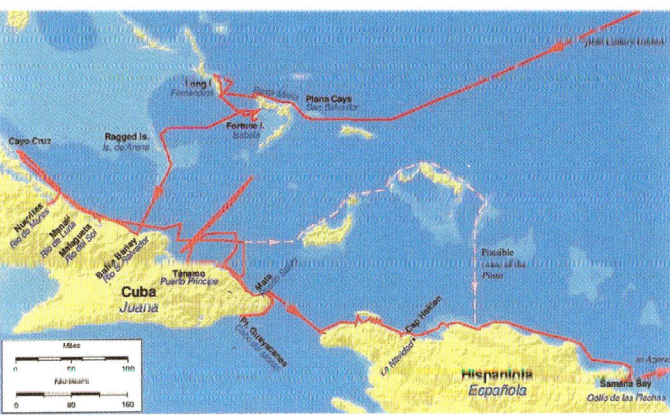

A map showing the transatlantic routes of the four voyages of Columbus. Image from original map – Viajes de Colon.

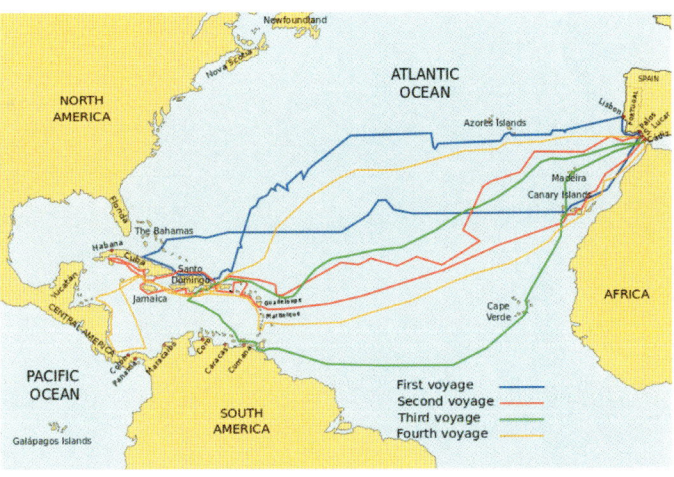

Map: Ten possible landfalls that Columbus could have reached during his first voyage as depicted in the white circles. Investigator Keith Pickering has selected Plana Cays as the most likely candidate. *Courtesy of Keith A. Pickering.*

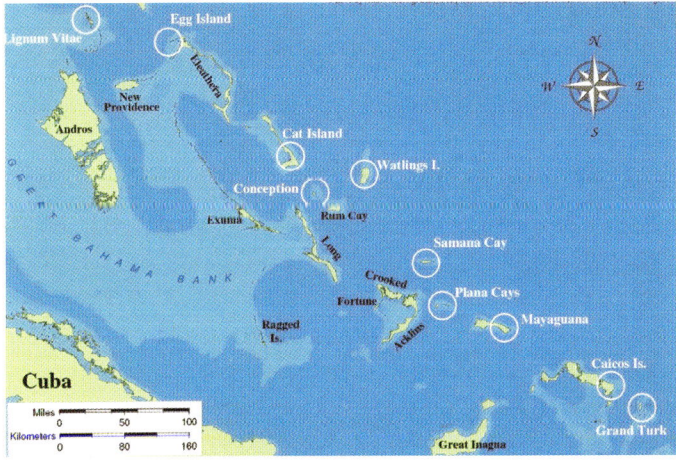

Map: First voyage of Columbus showing the five island landfalls (named by Columbus in blue-modern place names in black) made before Columbus reached Cuba and Hispaniola. San Salvador (Plana Cays) is thought to be Columbus's first landfall of the New World. *Courtesy of Keith A. Pickering.*

Second, Third & Fourth Voyages: September 1493-November 1504

On each of these voyages, Columbus, with expanded crews and better ships, continued his exploration throughout the Caribbean, and established a permanent settlement in Hispaniola. He was the first European since Leif Ericson to set foot on the mainland of the Americas (Venezuela), additionally visiting Mexico, Honduras, Panama, and Jamaica. In between his third and fourth voyages, Columbus was imprisoned for awhile due to his mismanagement as Governor of the Indies and his alleged atrocities of Native Americans in order to maintain control and expedite the conversion to Christianity of non-believers.

Two years after his last voyage, Columbus, now a broken and ill man, passed away at the age of fifty-four in 1506. Naturally, a controversy has ensued as to where Columbus's remains are buried, as they were removed many times. DNA analysis suggests Seville, Southern Spain, but similar remains are buried in Santo Domingo, Dominican Republic.

Today we celebrate Columbus Day, not because Christopher Columbus was traditionally considered to be the first to discover America, but because his legacy was that through his explorations he was the first to establish Western civilization in the Americas. The lands that Columbus discovered were not India as he always believed, but a new continent verified by the explorations of Amerigo Vespucci in 1502-1504. The leading cartographer of that era, Martin Waldseemuller, was so convinced that when he published an updated map of the world in 1507, he designated the new continent as America, which has stood the test of time.

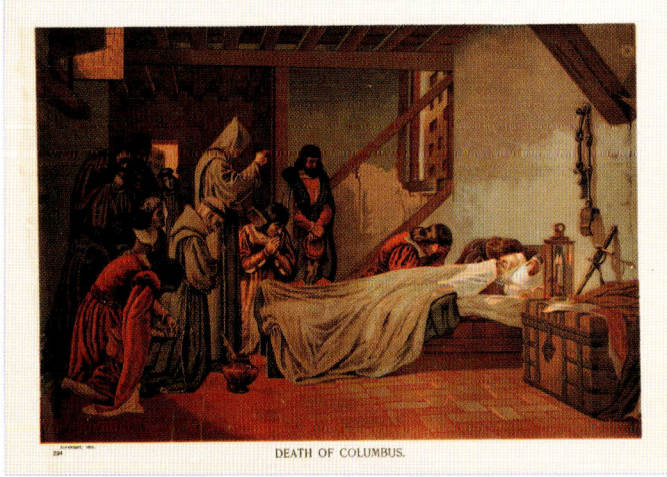

Antique Color Bookplate: Plate No. 4: Death of Columbus (at Valladolid, Crown of Castile, Spain). *From the book Columbus and Columbia, published in 1893 by the Historical Publishing Company, Philadelphia.*

Chapter 8

Labor Day

LABOR DAY is a United States legal federal holiday observed on the first Monday in September. It celebrates the long history of the labor movement as well as the economic and social achievements and contributions of the American worker.

In mid-nineteenth century United States, there was much labor strife between management and the working people. Typical non-unionized workers had a litany of complaints against management: (1) child labor; (2) long hours; (3) many times being responsible for providing their own working materials; (4) low pay; (5) introduction of labor-saving machinery; and (6) oppressive and unsafe working conditions. Due to these repressive conditions, many trade unions were formed, but most did not have the staying power to successfully challenge management. After the conclusion of the American Civil War in 1865, war veterans, freed black men, women, and children all vied for job opportunities, especially in the North, which saw the rapid industrialization of the metals industry, coal mining, and the building trades, as well as the expansion of railroads throughout the country.

Due to the many trades that the growth and expansion of America depended upon, it was thought that combining many similar trades under one federation would have greater bargaining power. Therefore, in 1866, the National Labor Union was founded, which was the first national labor federation in the United States. In 1867, a new labor union, Order of the Knights of St. Crispin, was founded in New England for skilled shoemakers. By 1870, with 50,000 members, it was the largest union in the country. Due to ineffectual management, both of these federations eventually failed.

First Day Cover: Labor Day "The First Monday in September" Dated Camden, New Jersey, September 3, 1956. Cachet created by The Aristocrats. Close up of cachet drawing.

Labor Day Souvenirs: "Labor conquers everything – The strictest law oft becomes the severest injustice" and "Service shall with steeled sinews toil, and labour will refresh itself with hope." Publisher is unknown; "Labor Day Series" No. 1.

Organized in 1869 in Philadelphia by members of a tailor's union, the Knights of Labor became the first effective labor organization with a national perspective. The Knights enjoyed a fifteen-year growth spurt based on the fact that as membership expanded the organization became less fraternal (promoting the social and cultural uplift of the working man) and functioned more like a labor union in that they began to aid various strikes and boycotts. Eventually the Knights began to initiate strikes based on their demands for an eight-hour day. One of the more successful strikes early in the Knights history was leading 200,000 railway workers to a marginal victory over the "Robber Baron" Jay Gould and his Southwestern Railway System. By 1886 the Knights were trying to coordinate 1,400 strikes involving over 600,000 workers nationwide throughout many trades; these strikes involved both peaceful and violent confrontations. All of this frenetic activity was accomplished prior to the invention of the telephone, which was a quick way of providing rapid communication over distances by the use of paired telephones.

169

The McCormick Reaper Factory Strike

In May 1886, one of the most memorable strikes in labor history was initiated by the Knights of Labor against the McCormick Reaper Factory in Chicago, Illinois. The strike, for an eight-hour working day, had worldwide implications. During the strike a confrontation ensued between the striking workers and the company's strikebreakers who were protected by the police. At the end of the day, the striking workers surged towards the "scabs" and police fired into the crowd, killing at least two McCormick workers. As there was outrage against this police "brutality," local anarchists seized the moment by printing and distributing fliers calling for a rally the following day at Haymarket Square in mid-town Chicago. The May 4th nighttime rally was peaceful and when it ended the police began to disperse the crowd in an orderly fashion. At that point an unknown person threw a pipe bomb toward the police, killing one. The police then indiscriminately fired into the crowd, killing not only seven more of their own but four workers as well. An investigation into the bloody riot caused the conviction of eight anarchists, of which four were eventually hanged in November 1887. While the Knights of Labor were not directly involved, the labor federation was seriously hurt by the false accusations of anarchist's leanings. In the end, the Haymarket affair was a setback for the American labor movement.

The period of the 1880s in America was a time of exceptional economic expansion, driven by railroad speculation and ending with railroad overbuilding and shaky financing that culminated in the Panic of 1893 and the attendant double-digit unemployment rate between 17% and 19%. Failures of more than five hundred banks occurred due to the run on the banks as well as the bankruptcy of 15,000 companies and three major railroads, all of which contributed to one of the worst depressions in United States economic history.

The American labor movement took note of this prosperity and depression and sought to strengthen its aims by filling a vacuum. In 1881, the Federation of Organized Trades and Labor Unions began under the leadership of Samuel Gompers with the original goals of encouragement of the formation of trade unions, a national eight-hour work day, the prohibition of child labor (finally outlawed in 1938), and the exclusion of foreign contract workers. In 1886, the relationship between the federated trade union movement and the Knights of Labor dramatically worsened due to

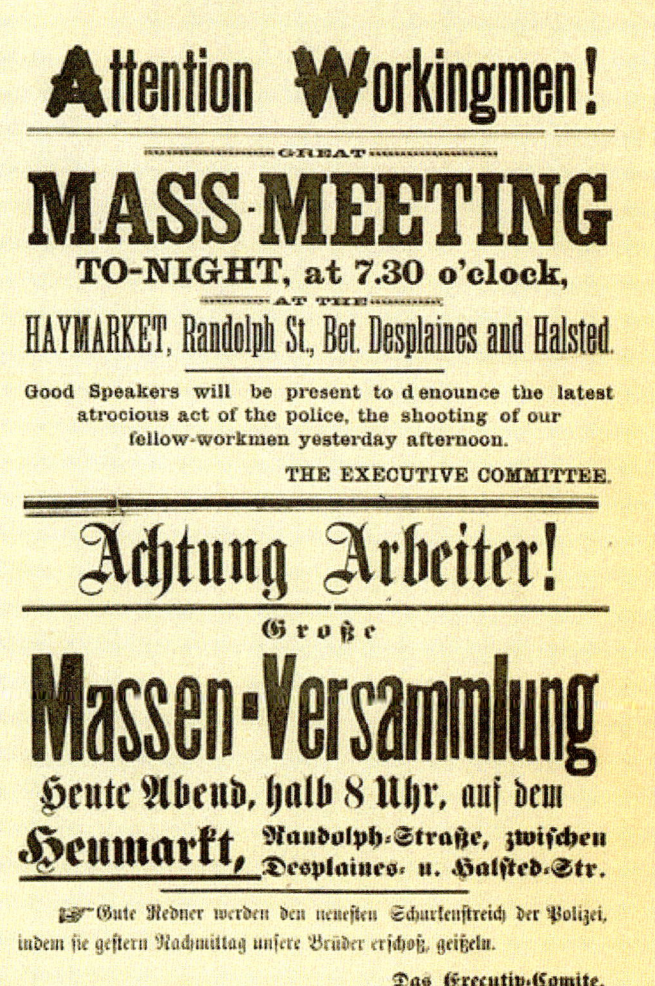

This bilingual English-German flier notified people of a rally in support of striking workers at Haymarket Square on May 4, 1886. From the Chicago History Museum collection of artifacts pertinent to the Haymarket Affair.

"The violent confrontation between Chicago police and labor protesters in 1886 proved to be a pivotal setback in the struggle for American workers' rights." Advertisement from the Chicago History Museum collection of artifacts pertinent to the Haymarket Affair.

their alleged role in the Haymarket Affair. Therefore, on December 8, 1886, a forced merger between the FOTLU and the Knights occurred resulting in the formation of the American Federation of Labor, which still exists today.

In the early formative days of the prior Federation of Organized Trades, a proposal was offered by Peter J. McGuire of the Carpenters Union (Knights of Labor member) to initiate a national Labor Day holiday on the first Monday in September as a celebration of "the strength and spirit of the American worker." It was McGuire's intent to have the workers enjoy a "festive day to parade through the streets of the city" and so on September 5, 1882, 30,000 marchers paraded down New York's Fifth Avenue to Union Square, resulting in the nation's first Labor Day celebration honoring the working classes of America. The event was so successful that workers around the country adopted the idea. In 1887, Oregon became the first state to legislate Labor Day a legal holiday. Over the next seven years, by 1894, thirty other states adopted the idea.

Haymarket Martyr's Monument: Five convicted anarchists were buried here after their hanging (and one by suicide) November 11, 1887. On the monument are the etched words uttered by Albert Spies before his death… "The day will come when our silence will be more powerful then the voices you are throttling today." Monument dedicated June 25, 1893, and is located at the Forest Home Cemetery, Chicago, Illinois.

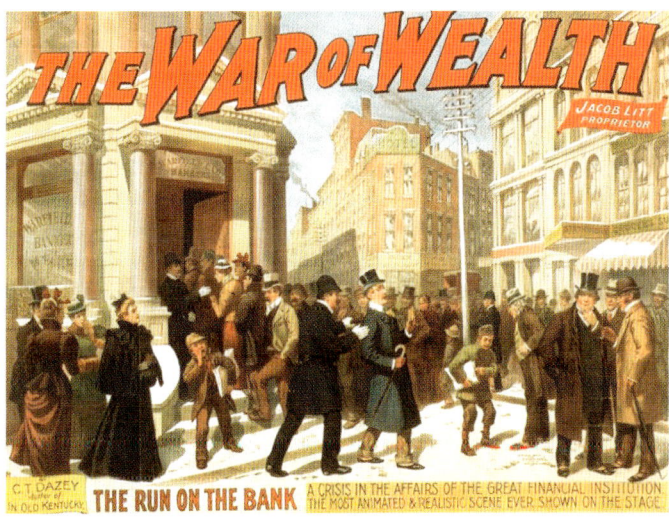

Poster for the play "The War of Wealth" written by Charles Turner Dazey. The advertisement read "The Run on the Bank…a crisis in the affairs of the great financial institution…" The play opened in February 1895 based on the "Panic of 1893." Sounds familiar!

History Flash Card: Life in America with "The first Labor Day Parade in New York City in 1882" as an illustration.

The Pullman Palace Car Company Strike

From May 11 to August 3, 1894, at the Pullman Palace Car Company, Chicago, Illinois, one of the greatest strikes in American history occurred consisting of 250,000 workers. Pullman, Illinois, was a company town, founded in 1880 by George Pullman, President of the railroad sleeping car company. Pullman designed and built the town to stand as a utopian workers' community and all of its residents worked for the Pullman Company. When the Panic of 1893 occurred, the resultant depression caused Pullman to suffer a decline of railroad car orders that ultimately forced him to lay off hundreds of employees. Those who retained their jobs suffered pay cuts while the rents on their company housing stayed the same. This set of circumstances caused the employees to walk out demanding some combination of higher wages and lower rents. The American Railway Union, led by Socialist Eugene V. Debs, came to the cause of the striking workers. The local strike now became a national crisis as all railroads that were carrying Pullman cars were boycotted. Soon after, violence occurred with rioting, pillaging, and burning of Pullman cars executed by strikers and non-strikers alike. President Grover Cleveland declared the strike a federal crime and deployed 12,000 troops to quell the strikers. This prompted more violence and resulted in the death of two men, after which the strike was broken. Eugene Debs was sent to prison, his American Railway Union disbanded, and all Pullman employees had to sign a new anti-strike pledge.

In 1894, which was an election year, President Glover Cleveland was the brunt of many protests concerning his harsh methods in breaking the Pullman strike. Therefore, in a conciliatory mood, the President sought to appease the national workers by making legislation a top priority of granting workers a paid holiday. On June 24, 1894, Congress passed an act making Labor Day a legal Federal holiday to be held on the first Monday in September of each year for all fifty states, the District of Columbia, and all territories.

The addition of Labor Day to the federal holiday calendar did not forestall the continuation of strikes in America. It was only when the United States was building up its stockpiles of war-related goods both for the Allies as well as for America's eventual entrance into World War I that strikes, in the name of patriotism, abated due to no-strike pledges.

The Pullman Car Company's striking workers stand outside the Arcade Building in Pullman, Chicago, in 1894. The Illinois National Guard is guarding the building against vandalism. Abraham Lincoln Historical Digitization Project. Author unknown.

The Anthracite Coal Strike

The largest strike to occur subsequent to the annual Labor Day holiday events was the Great Anthracite Coal Strike of 1902. Prior to this, it was recognized that coal mining was a very dangerous business due to the extreme occupational hazards that one endured, especially when child labor was involved. In 1890, the United Mine Workers of America (UMWA) was formed by the amalgamation of the National Progressive Union (just two years old) and the miners' locals under the Knights of Labor. This was an industrial union that represented all workers in the massive coal industry, whether it be bituminous (soft coal) or anthracite (hard coal). Being an affiliate of the AFL helped this new amalgamated union win important strikes in 1894 and 1897, creating the eight-hour workday. These strikes helped the UMWA gain important membership (115,000 members); it also received recognition and acceptance from the Bituminous Coal operators as a bargaining body.

In 1902, the UMWA decided to strike against the Anthracite mine owners whose mines were located in the coalfields of Eastern Pennsylvania. The goals of the UMWA were to gain some control over this industry due to the hazardous working conditions, asking for higher wages, and shorter workdays, as well as the very important need for union recognition. This strike occurred on May 2, 1902, with approximately 140,000 miners walking off their jobs. Anthracite coal, due to its higher heat value and less smoke, was extremely important to the well-being of millions of people who need a constant supply of coal during the winter months to heat their homes as there was no suitable substitute. Soon some violence occurred between the strikers and the strikebreakers bolstered by the Pennsylvania National Guard and various police agencies. With no resolution in sight, and winter fast approaching, President Theodore Roosevelt convened a coalition of representatives from the government, labor, and management on October 2, 1902. Within three weeks, this commission was able to overcome most of the roadblocks, and the UMWA signaled the miners to return back to the coal mines on October 23, 1902, ending this strike after 163 days. The compromise included a ten percent wage increase instead of twenty percent, a nine-hour workday instead of the prevailing ten-hour standard, but due to industry refusal, no formal recognition of the UMWA.

One year after World War I was over, the UMWA announced a strike for November 1, 1919, the date selected perhaps to intimidate management into acquiescing to increased wage demands due to the need for ensuring supplies of heating coal for the winter. Toward the end of World War I, the Bolshevik's formulated a revolution in Russia initiating a Soviet-Communist regime. Management used smear tactics implying that the strike was Communist financed and led. After the strike dragged on for two more weeks, public sentiment was against the strike and the UMWA quietly called off this action and an agreement was signed on December 10, 1919. It was not until the next year that anthracite coal mine owners realized that the UMWA would not go away, so, in 1920, a formal agreement was signed extending formal recognition to the UMWA. One sad note was that the UMWA could not force the end of child labor or strictly enforce prevailing child labor laws. In many cases, young boys worked with their fathers in the same mine, which helped increase the amount of coal mined as the miners were paid per pound of coal. Eventually, in 1938, President Franklin Delano Roosevelt signed the Fair Labor Standards Act, which placed limits on many forms of child labor except in agriculture.

A lone miner enters the mouth of a slope mine with the sides and ceiling held up solely by wooden timbers that could collapse at a moment's notice. Entrance to a West Virginia coal mine, September 1908. Photo by Lewis Hine.

Puck, October 1902: Cartoon is based on the "Great Anthracite Coal Strike" of 1902 depicting a disgruntled UMWA miner striking out at a worried mine owner.

Los Angeles Times, November 22, 1919: The cartoon "Keeping Warm" depicts Uncle Sam getting tired of the endless strikes especially in the coal industry when winter is approaching.

The Lawrence Textile Strike

Labor unrest, with a child labor component, prevailed in 1912 when the Lawrence Textile Strike, often known as the "Bread and Roses" strike, was started by dozens of immigrant communities totaling 20,000 largely female workers in Lawrence, Massachusetts, under the leadership of the radical Industrial Workers of the World. Work was grueling and dangerous in textile mills due to the pace of activity, and nearly fifty perent of all workers in four mills of the American Woolen Company, as an example, were girls between the ages of 14 and 18. The average workweek hours of fifty-four were for both women and children. The mortality rate for children at age six was 50% due to the lack of nutritious food as the money earned only went so far. This strike, which ended in March, pitted the mill owners, the militia, and the AFL-sponsored United Textile Workers against the IWW. Some of the textile mills were torched and caches of dynamite were found. The gains derived from the strike largely dissipated over the next few years as the IWW union collapsed due to its radical taint and was not able to provide any more help.

In the period from the start of organized labor and the recognition of workers' rights in the late 1880s to the World War I years, many cities and towns, large and small, promoted parades in order to improve visibility of the labor movement. Today, political speeches are more the norm, along with the last chance to go to the beach, family get-togethers, and picnics before summer ends and school begins…along with a new football season.

Iconic picture of barely educated young boys working twelve-hour days, six days a week at a Pennsylvania coal mine with no sick days, holidays, or pensions. Breathing coal dust destroyed their lungs by their middle age. Image from National Archives and Records Administration.

Puck, August 1912: Centerfold illustration of "Lady Liberty" unsheathing her "law and order" sword to protect a worker against violent strikers. Some strikers became very violent, torching management buildings and attacking fellow workers who were not striking. This harmed the mission of the Labor Movement.

Labor Day Parade at Rochester, New York. Color-tinted postcard published by *The Rochester News Company*, early 1900s.

The New Yorker, September 6, 1993. Artist: Unknown. The Labor Day vendor is looking for his last customer of the summer.

Labor Day parade at a rural location of Cherokee, Oklahoma. The clock read 8:18 a.m. on Labor Day of 1908. Color-tinted postcard. Publisher unknown.

Chapter 9

Flag Day

FLAG DAY, unlike Federally mandated official holidays, is celebrated as an annual public holiday on June 14th. The first instance of this was in 1916 when President Woodrow Wilson issued a proclamation that officially designated June 14th as Flag Day. In August 1949 National Flag Day was established by an Act of Congress under President Harry S. Truman's administration. The Congress also designated various United States federal observances of which, besides Flag Day, are patriotic celebrations such as Patriot Day (September 11th), Constitution/Citizenship Day (September 17th), and Pearl Harbor Remembrance Day (December 7th). In the United States Flag Day commemorates the adoption of the national flag of the United States. On June 14, 1937 Pennsylvania became the first — and is still the only one — state to celebrate Flag Day as a state holiday.

"There is always a clinging to the land of one's birth": Proud to be an American as the flag flies high. Published by Franz Huld.

Woodrow Wilson pictured with the "Flag he loves is the flag that you love." Publisher is unknown; "Flag" Series No. 4.

Early Beginnings of National Flag Day

The earliest reference to the "suggestion" of a Flag Day observation was credited to George Morris of Hartford, Connecticut, on June 14, 1861. According to *The Daily Courant* editorial: "Today is the Anniversary of the American Flag. It has been suggested that the day be hereafter celebrated in a quiet way by a general display of flags." On June 17, 1862, the Connecticut State Legislature passed the first Flag Day Resolution in honor of the "85th Anniversary of our Country's Banner." Much of the American Civil War patriotic sheet music showed vivid images of the flag and with other national emblems.

"The American Flag" sheet music cover. Words are by J. H. Drake and music by Bellini. Respectfully dedicated to Major general Winfield Scott. 1863.

"Our Banner of Glory" music sheet cover. A National Hymn: Words by G. W. Cutter, Esq. and arranged by W. C. Peters, 1862.

On June 14, 1885, Bernard J. Cigrand, a grade school teacher, was credited for holding the first recognized formal observance of Flag Day at his school in Waubeka, Wisconsin. This observance commemorated Congress' adoption of the Stars and Stripes as the flag of the United States on June 14, 1777. After this time, Cigrand spent long years of devoted effort to bring about the national recognition and observance of Flag Day. His efforts paid off when, on May 30, 1916, President Wilson issued a proclamation calling for a nationwide observance of Flag Day, which occurred two weeks later. Less than a year later, the United States would be thrust into World War I in comradeship with other Allied powers. Many patriotic posters and postcards of that era showed feminine icons such as Lady Liberty rallying around the flag.

"Triumph of Democracy" as the flags of Belgium, France, Italy, the United Kingdom, the United States, and Russia proudly stand together. Published by E. de Villeneuve.

Two postcards depicting Lady Liberty: With the eagle and flag – "Our Emblems of Liberty" (published by Julius Bien & Co.; "Flag" Series No. 710) and in her white flowing gown holding the fluttering flag (Publisher is unknown).

1917 Poster: "The Flag of Freedom" is held high by an Army Corps nurse while a platoon of soldiers marching off to war parade by, surrounded by the symbols of freedom, such as the Liberty Bell and the Statue of Liberty. *From the author's private collection.*

The week of June 14th of any year is designated as "National Flag Week." During National Flag Week the President will issue a proclamation urging all United States citizens to fly the American flag for the duration of the week. Also the National Flag Day Foundation holds an annual observance for Flag Day on the second Sunday in June. The usual program includes a ceremonial raising the flag, recitation of the Pledge of Allegiance, singing patriotic songs such as The Star Spangled Banner as well as hosting a parade. One of the popular locations to attend a Flag Day observation has been the Betsy Ross House in Philadelphia, Pennsylvania.

To the present day, there have been sustained efforts to continue to promote Flag Day observations. One problem is that school is out during the summer break so there is little chance to involve our nation's children in the history and etiquette of the flag. Also, Independence Day celebrations are just three weeks off so there is some merging of both observations. In an article in *The New York Times* dated June 13, 2011, the writer opines that: "Today, exactly 150 years ago after [Flag Day] was first celebrated, almost no one seems to have noticed the anniversary. Google searches for 'Sesquicentennial of Flag Day' …yield exactly zero hits." The writer goes on to state that "the holiday's popularity seems to have crested in the periods of the two world wars…and for the 1960s generation, it became more or less the epitome of square: a vaguely embarrassing grade-school memory." He closes with an upbeat assessment that "this June 14th — as on all other days of the year — the American flag remains as ubiquitous and as venerated as the most pious citizen of Hartford could have wished in 1861."

Chalkware figure: A red-haired cadet dressed in her military uniform with silver hat and boots carries the American flag. 14" high.

The "Star-Spangled Banner" lyrics honor the flag in these three postcards. Gold stars provide the background in one published by International Art Publishing Co.; a young lady with a blue headband with white stars "And the star spangled banner in triumph shall wave O'er the land of the free and the home of the brave!" (published by Arthur Livingston); and a wreath of flowers decorate the flag (published by Tuck & Sons as part of "Decoration Day" Series No. 107).

First card: A waving flag on a flagpole is the central image as it overlooks the sunset. "…Wide spread thy folds and gather safe, The men of various warring creeds." The lower part of the card shows a bucolic sailing scene bracketed by two vertical banners. Artist signed Chapman. Published by International Art Publishing Co. Second card: Publisher is unknown; part of "Decoration Day" Series No. 1.

Raggedy Ann (15" in height) and Raggedy Andy (16" in height) Dolls, based on the creation by artist and storyteller Johnny Gruelle, 1915. Part of Salute to Libery Series. Made by Applause, LLC., CA.

A young boy draped in the flag salutes: "I'm wrapt up in my Country and You." Published by Bergman; No. 8350.

The U. S. Flag: Origin and Design

It took from 1607 to 1733, a period of 126 years, to finally form the Thirteen Colonies of British North America into three sections: New England Colonies, Middle Colonies, and Southern Colonies. Thereafter each of the colonies had their own separate flag. By April 1775, the American Revolutionary War had begun. The First Continental Congress was looking for a suitable national emblem that personified the one, undividable union of the original thirteen colonies. While it is not known for sure who designed the first national flag of the United States, it resembled current British red ensign flags. This flag which was named the Grand Union Flag (or the Continental Colors) consisted of thirteen horizontal stripes, seven red and six white, with the British Union Flag of the time located in the canton. The Grand Union Flag was first hoisted over the very first ship of the new Continental navy, the 24-gun frigate *Alfred*, in Philadelphia on December 2, 1775. The Commander of this new ship was Lt. John Paul Jones.

First Day of Issue: Colonial Flags, dated July 4, 1968. A set of ten U. S. 6-cent postage stamps were issued and placed on thick paper accompanied with attractive red, blue, and black pen and ink engraved drawings of various American Revolutionary battle scenes. The stamps are (1) First Navy Jack (Don't Tread On Me), 1775; (2) Washington's Cruiser Flag, 1775; (3) Rhode Island Flag, 1775; (4) Philadelphia Light Horse Flag, 1775; (5) Bunker Hill Flag, 1775; (6) Grand Union Flag, 1776; (7) Fort Moultrie Flag, 1776; (8) Bennington Flag, 1777; (9) First Stars and Stripes, 1777; and (10) U. S. Flag, 1795-1818 (Fort McHenry Flag).

John Paul Jones was one of the leading naval heroes of the Revolutionary War. Throughout most of the war, Jones, as Commander of the Ranger, attacked British merchant shipping as well as Royal Navy frigates. In 1779, the now Captain Jones took command of the 42-gun Bonhomme Richard sailing off of Great Britain's coast. There Jones and his five ship squadron met up with a large merchant convoy protected by the 50-gun British frigate, the HMS Serapis, and a smaller ship. The Serapis engaged the Bonhomme Richard. At one point the British commander asked if Jones was ready to strike their colors but Jones uttered that now famous quote, "I have not yet begun to fight!" Eventually the tide of the battle went to Jones and the Commander of the Serapis finally surrendered. For this famous victory, John Paul Jones was awarded a commemorative gold medal by Congress in 1787.

The Grand Union Flag was also raised by General George Washington's Army on New Year's Day, 1776 near his headquarters at Cambridge, Massachusetts. Throughout 1776 and into early 1777 the Grand Union Flag was used by the Continental Army as both a naval ensign and garrison flag. The Second Continental Congress through the Flag Act of (June 14th) 1777 enacted a resolution "that the Flag of the United States be 13 stripes alternate red and white, that the Union be 13 stars white in a blue field representing a new constellation." The first official national flag known as the "Stars and Stripes" became into existence due to Congressional approval.

Who made the very first American Flag? Stamped into the consciousness of every school boy and girl is the answer — Betsy Ross! Betsy Ross was born into a Quaker family on January 1, 1752 as the eighth of seventeen children. Through her marriage she became an expert seamstress and upholsterer repairing uniforms and making tents and blankets. According to popular legend, Betsy Ross, at age 25, was asked to make the first American flag based on the dimensions approved by Congress. The story of Betsy Ross and the American flag got its start from a paper presented to the Historical Society of Pennsylvania in 1870 (some ninety-three years removed from the "fact") by William J. Canby, Ross's grandson who claimed that his grandmother had "made with her hands the first flag" of the United States. This story began to gain some advocates at the time of the (United States) Centennial International Exhibition of 1876, which was the first official World's Fair in the United States, and held in Philadelphia, Pennsylvania from May 10th to November 10th. While the premise of the Exhibition was to celebrate the 100th Anniversary of the signing of the Declaration of Independence in Philadelphia, the true goal was to

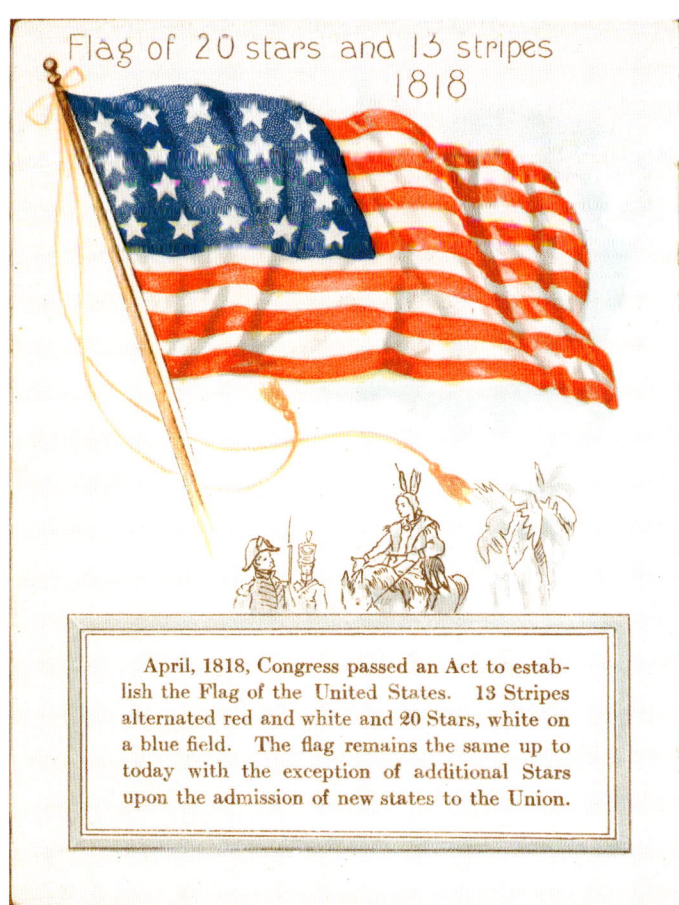

The History of the American Flag: This booklet contains ten pages, measuring 3-1/2" x 4-1/2". It was published in 1912 by Chase & Sanborn Tea and Coffee Importers. The nine flags illustrated are (front to back): 1. New England Colonial Flag, 1686; 2. Taunton Flag (Liberty & Union), 1774; 3. Bunker Hill Flag, 1775; 4. Pine Tree Flag of the Navy, 1775; 5. Rattlesnake Flag (Don't Tread On Me), 1776; 6. Crescent Flag (Liberty), 1776; 7. Grand Union Flag, 1776; 8. Betsy Ross Flag, 1777; and 9. Flag of 20 Stars and 13 Stripes, 1818.

showcase to the world the United States' industrial and innovative prowess which included Alexander Graham Bell's telephone. While there was no direct mention of Betsy Ross and her making of the first American flag, there was an indirect tie-in due to the patriotic premise of the Centennial as well as Philadelphia being her home (and a tourist attraction) and final resting place. It was at that time after the Centennial that the apocryphal story of General George Washington and two representatives from the Continental Congress visited Ross at her upholstery shop to discuss with her the making of a flag from their rough design (thought to be one by Francis Hopkinson). While there is little credence to support this story, Betsy Ross was one of several flag makers in Philadelphia and had already made a colonial flag for Pennsylvania. Betsy Ross was probably consulted and her contribution was to change the 6-pointed stars to the easier to cut 5-pointed stars. She passed away in 1836 at the age of 84, and her home, the Betsy Ross House, is one of the most visited tourist attractions in Philadelphia. This is a good story of our first flag and, since there have been no others to come forward to claim construct, celebrate Betsy Ross for the work she could have done!

After Vermont and Kentucky, the 14th and 15th states, were added to the Union in 1791 and 1792, respectively, two more stars and two more stripes were added to the national flag in 1795. Even though three more states (Tennessee, Ohio and Louisiana) achieved statehood by the War of 1812, it was this 15-star, 15-stripe flag that became the "star-spangled banner," which, in 1814, Francis Scott Key was inspired to write in celebration of the fact that this flag was still flying over Fort McHenry the morning after suffering bombardment from British naval vessels. In December 1818, after five more states gained admittance, totaling 21, Congress passed legislation fixing the background of the number of stripes at 13 (for the original 13 colonies) — seven red and six white, and requiring that the number of stars on the canton equal the number of states. Even during the American Civil War, the Federal Government found time to admit two new states: West Virginia, 35th in 1863, and Nevada, 36th in 1864. After Arizona, the 48th, was admitted in 1912, the flag stayed constant with 48 stars in the canton. When Hawaii was admitted to the Union on August 21, 1959 as the 50th state, the last new star was added to the flag on July 4, 1960.

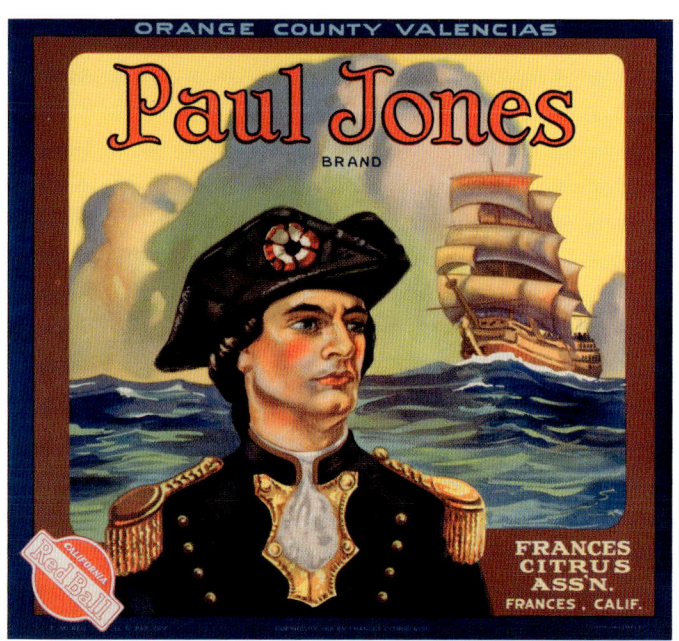

Crate Label: "(John) Paul Jones" brand. Frances Citrus Ass'n, Frances, California.

"Betsy Ross Making the First American Flag 1778": A scene bracketed by a firecracker. Published by Tuck & Sons; "Independence Day" Series No. 159.

"The Birth of Old Glory" by Edward Percy Moran (1862-1935), painter of American historical scenes. This image from 1917 depicts what is presumed to be Betsy Ross and two children presenting the "Betsy Ross flag" to George Washington and three other men.

Three postcards capture the history of the Betsy Ross Flag: (1) "Betsy Ross making the first flag with stars and stripes" shown with George Washington and another gentleman. Published by Winsch; (2) "Washington adopting the five-pointed Star" for the flag's canton. Publisher is unknown; part of "Washington Birthday" Series No. 1; and (3) Betsy Ross House, "Birthplace of Old Glory," Philadelphia, Pennsylvania. Publisher is unknown.

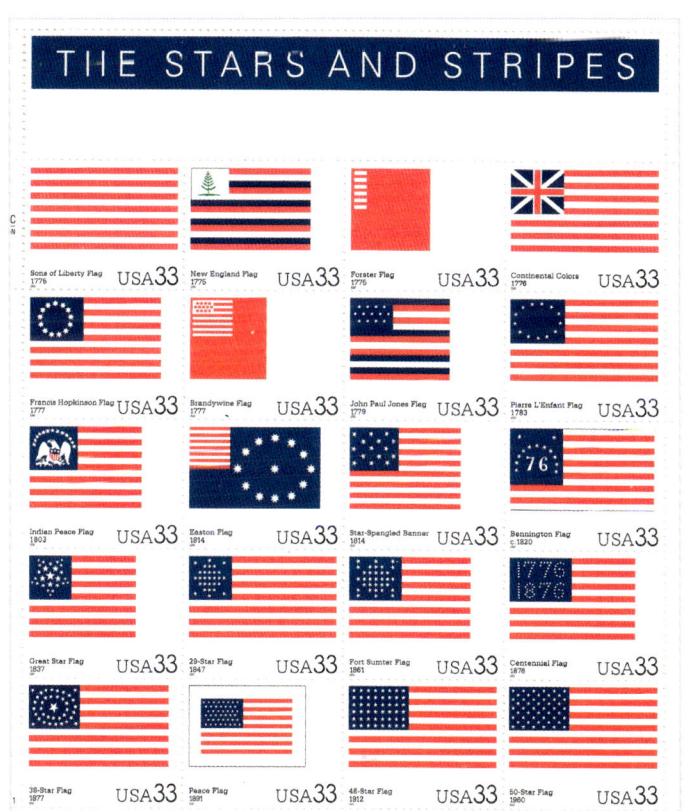

A pane of 33-cent stamps issued in 1999: "The Stars and Stripes" featuring the history of the flag through twenty versions, starting from the Sons of Liberty flag in 1775 to the 50-Star Flag in 1960. History of each flag is on the reverse of the pane.

185

"Long may she wave!" Two "real" women were photographed in matching long dresses and hats and superimposed on the cards, waving the flag/banner. Notice the flags have forty-four stars. The publisher is unknown.

"By land and sea, it shall ever be Old Glory." A naval ship patrols the waters while a soldier patrols his camp beneath the waving flag. Published by Julius Bien; "Flag" Series No. 710.

At the time of the Spanish-American War of 1896, the only way for friends to communicate their patriotism by mail was through the use of flag images on regular mailing envelopes that contained many patriotic sayings and verses. While the telephone was in limited use, postcards were still just a few years away from being the next big communication application.

U. S. Flag Etiquette

While flag etiquette is outside the scope of this book, you can refer to the U. S. Code, Title 4 (Flag & Seal, Seat of Government), Chapter 1 (The Flag), Sections 1-10 (as well as the many online sites expressly set up to advise a person on this): (1) Rules for Display; (2) Rules for Display with other Flags; (3) Admonitions that the Flag is a symbol not a decoration; (4) Rules for flying the Flag at Half-Staff; (5) Rules for Washing, Repairing and/or Disposal; (6) Rules for Folding the Flag; (7) Rules for Carrying the Flag; (8) Suggestions for Proper Fabrics and Exposure; (9) Suggestions for Flagpole sizes and length; and (10) Rules on When and How to Fly the Flag. Another very useful website for information regarding the United States Flag is: www.usflag.org. Because the red, white and blue color combinations are very attractive complementary colors, there are literally thousands of patriotic items made to emulate the flag's colors, and there are books devoted to this subject. But discretion is called for and, according to the U. S. Flag Code, many items are restricted in their use of the flag image.

Eight Spanish-American Patriotic Covers illustrated with multi-color designs and patriotic verses: "If anyone attempts to haul down the American flag, shoot him on the spot" and "Our Country! – May she be always right, but right or wrong, Our Country!"

Red Star Line Folding Fan, circa 1900, made of printed paper and wood, 8.5" x 16" x 1". This could have been a give-away souvenir at an Independence Day celebration in hot July. *Courtesy of Kit Hinrichs/Studio Hinrichs. Photographer: Terry Heffernan.*

Embroidered Wall Hanging: "Old Glory–Long May It Wave." Handmade, 15" x 16". Artist unknown, c. 1940s.

Stick Fans, c. 1900-1945, made of printed paper and wood, were handed out by local merchants at many various patriotic celebrations. *Courtesy of Kit Hinrichs/Studio Hinrichs. Photographer: Terry Heffernan.*

Various patriotic collectibles – Uncle Sam coin bank, Uncle Sam pencil box, Fourth of July parade dress, patriotic buttons, hood ornament, folding fan, bicentennial bow tie, Shirley Temple mirror, brass and enamel belt buckle – all in vivid red, white, and blue. *Courtesy of Kit Hinrichs/Studio Hinrichs. Photographer: Terry Heffernan.*

"SHIPROCK." Painting depicting a Navajo woman draped in an American Flag at sunrise. Presentation proof viii/x. Serigraph print by the late R. C. (Rudolph Carl) Gorman, 2001. 30" x 23". *From the author's personal collection.*

Crownpoint Pictorial Navajo Handwoven Rug, 29" x 48," purchased at Tobe Turpen's Indian Trading Company, Gallup, New Mexico, c. 1974.

These handmade patriotic pillows are each decorated with an American flag image – "Old Glory" and "Stars and Stripes Forever."

The Pledge of Allegiance

The original Pledge of Allegiance was written by Francis Bellamy, a Baptist minister, and published in the September 8, 1892, issue of the Boston-based *The Youth's Companion*. Interestingly, this Pledge was inserted into an advertisement for a celebration of the 400-year-anniversary, October 12, 1892, of Columbus' discovery of America. Since Bellamy's original Pledge, four more changes to the wording have been made in order to make it more specific and unique to the United States. The initial 1892 version is:

> *"I pledge allegiance to my flag*
> *And the Republic for which it stands,*
> *One nation, indivisible,*
> *With liberty and justice for all"*

Timeline of changes to the Pledge of Allegiance

1892: A small wording change was made — "And to the Republic…"

1923: A major addition was made — "I pledge allegiance to the Flag of the United States and to the Republic…"

1924: A minor addition was made — "Of the United States of America and to the Republic…"

1954: A controversial addition was made — "One Nation under God, indivisible…"

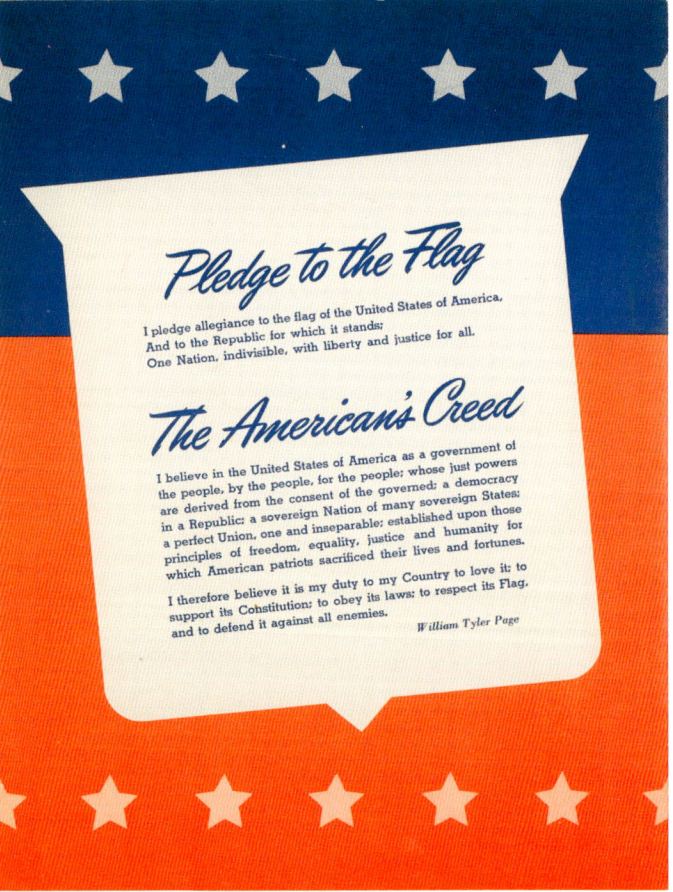

"I Pledge Allegiance": A Patriotic Album for All Americans. Song book contains eight patriotic songs with full stanzas and accompanied by vivid imagery. The booklet's back cover is printed with the Pledge of Allegiance and The American's Creed. Published 1941.

From 1948 until the Pledge was modified in 1954, there was an up swell of support to add the words…"under God" to the verse. With President Dwight David Eisenhower's backing, Congress passed the necessary legislation and Eisenhower signed the bill into law on Flag Day, June 14, 1954. In 1942 the Pledge of Allegiance was added to the U. S. Flag Code, Title 4, Chapter 1, and Section 4. Therefore the phrase "under God" was incorporated into the Pledge of Allegiance June 14, 1954, by a Joint Resolution of Congress amending Section 4 of the Flag Code enacted in 1942.

According to the U. S. Flag Code, the Pledge of Allegiance "should be rendered by standing at attention facing the flag with the right hand over the heart. When not in uniform men should remove their headdress with their right hand and hold it at the left shoulder, the hand being over the heart. Persons in uniform should remain silent, face the flag, and render the military salute." Also if there is no flag present, the Pledge should not be recited.

A final thought about the nation's flag written in 1861 by Henry Ward Beecher (1813-1887), prominent Congregationalist minister, social reformer, abolitionist, and public speaker:

> *"Our flag carries American ideas, American history and American feelings. It is not a painted rag. It is a whole national history. It is the Constitution. It is the Government. It is the emblem of the sovereignty of the people. It is the NATION."*

Two postcards: (1) the American flag with the Pledge of Allegiance. Published by Tichnor Bros.; and (2) The "Guardians of Our Nation," representatives from our World War II Armed Forces bracket the flag and the Pledge of Allegiance. Published by MWM Color-Litho Postcards.

"O may its stars forever shine So bright that all may see To walk in Justice, Love, and Truth And Glorious Liberty." A recessed image depicting the American Flag and the American bald eagle. Publisher is unknown; "Patriotic" Series No. 252.

A beautiful mountain lake scene bracketed by two American flag banners associated with "My Country 'tis of thee, Sweet Land of liberty, Of thee I sing." Artist signed Ellen Clapsaddle. Published by International Art Publishing Co.; Series No. 4397.

Bibliography

Beeman, Richard. *Plain, Honest Men: The Making of the American Constitution*. New York, New York: Random House Trade Paperbacks, 2009.

Bergreen, Laurence. *Columbus: The Four Voyages*. New York, New York: Viking Penguin, 2011.

Borkan, Gary A. *World War I Posters*. Atglen, Pennsylvania: Schiffer Publishing, 2002.

Brands H. W. *American Colossus: The Triumph of Capitalism, 1865-1900*. New York, New York: Anchor Books-Random House, 2011.

Czulewicz, Gerald E. *The Foremost Guide to Uncle Sam Collectibles*. Paducah, Kentucky: Collector Books, 1995.

Erskine, John. *Uncle Sam in the Eyes of His Family*. Indianapolis, Indiana: The Bobbs-Merrill Company, 1930.

Grant, John and Ray Jones. *The War of 1812*. Buffalo, New York: Western New York Publish Broadcasting Association, 2011.

Hinrichs, Kit and Delphine Hirasuna. *Long May She Wave*. Berkeley, California: Ten Speed Press, 2001.

Jusserand, J. J. "Armistice Day and the American Battle Fields." *National Geographic Magazine*, November 1929.

Landau, Elaine. *Veterans Day: Remembering Our War Heroes*. Berkeley Heights, New Jersey: Enslow Publishers, Inc., 2002.

Marschall, Rick. *Bully! The Life and Times of Theodore Roosevelt*. Washington, D.C.: Regnery Publishing, Inc., 2011.

McCullough, David. *1776*. New York, New York: Simon & Schuster Paperbacks, 2005.

Persico, Joseph E. *11th Month, 11th Day, 11th Hour: Armistice Day, 1918*. New York, New York: Random House, 2004.

Raatma, Lucia. *The Battles of Lexington & Concord*. Minneapolis, Minnesota: Compass Point Books, 2004.

Schauffler, Robert Haven. *Our American Holidays Armistice Day*. New York, New York: Dodd, Mead and Company, 1931.

Schweikart, Larry and Michael Allen. *A Patriot's History of the United States*. New York, New York: Penguin Group, 2004.

Souter, Gerry and Janet. *Founding Fathers: The Shaping of America*. New York, New York: Metro Books, 2009.

The Timechart History of America. New York, New York: Barnes and Noble, 2003.

Wenzel, Lynn and Carol J. Binkowski. *I Hear America Singing*. New York, New York: Crown Publishers, Inc., 1989.